Kentucky Quilts 1800-1900

Dedicated to Kentucky's quiltmakers, known and anonymous

fig. 1. Nancy Miller Grider, shown in an 1899 tintype, was the creator of the Kentucky Sun quilt on the cover and Plate 1.

❊ *Plate 1. Star or sun variation,
a unique design. (Family's name for
this design: Kentucky Sun.) Pieced
quilt. Made by Nancy Miller
Grider. Russell County, Kentucky.
Circa 1880? Wool. 75" x 62".
Collection of Ida C. Walts.*

*This much-used quilt is unusual in a
number of ways. The material is a
type not often used, made of wool
weft on a cotton warp, but is not
one of the linsey-woolsey cotton and
wool cloths seen in late eighteenth-
and early nineteenth-century American quilts. The design is extraordinary. While a few organizing
elements have been used–the centered circle and the blue cross quar-
tering it, the red and green arms
extending into the corners–it is a
free and exuberant creation that uses
the whole surface in a very painterly
manner.*

*Its construction is more like the
randomness of a Crazy quilt than
any of the more ordered American
types, yet it has little to do with the
Crazy quilt convention. I have seen
one other quilt from the region
which in conception (large, boldly
organized, irregular pieces with a
rough organization of rays emanat-
ing from the center) and materials
(wool and cotton mixture) was similar to this. It too had been quickly
made with little regard for niceties
of stitching, edging, etc., coarse
quilts for cold nights. These design
and construction characteristics may
indicate that the quilt represents a
regional type rather than a single,
creative insight. But that does not
detract from its vital and strange
quality; one would not be surprised
to hear it was influenced by another
aesthetic tradition. It is in any case
of great interest, both because it is a
visual triumph and for its unusual
technical features.*

Kentucky Quilts 1800-1900

The Kentucky Quilt Project

Introduction and
Quilt Commentaries
by Jonathan Holstein

Historical Text
by John Finley

✳ *Plate 2. Log Cabin blocks arranged in a framed center pattern. Pieced quilt. Made by Mary Elizabeth Woods Thurman. Somerset, Kentucky. Circa 1885. Wool. 82" x 55". Collection of Claire Elizabeth (Betty) Thurman.*

A glorious and skillfully planned Log Cabin quilt that uses a restrained palette to good effect. The blocks use only three colors, the same color forming the light stripe in each block and those stripes joining where the blocks connect. This careful meshing creates a sophisticated play of forms across the surface. The overall pattern—a square within a rectangle—is a rare one in Log Cabin quilts; and I have never seen another with an extra band of design, which was probably meant to dress up the foot of the bed. A small percentage of Log Cabin quilts were made with just a few colors in their blocks precisely to make such interesting visual effects. They almost always succeed.

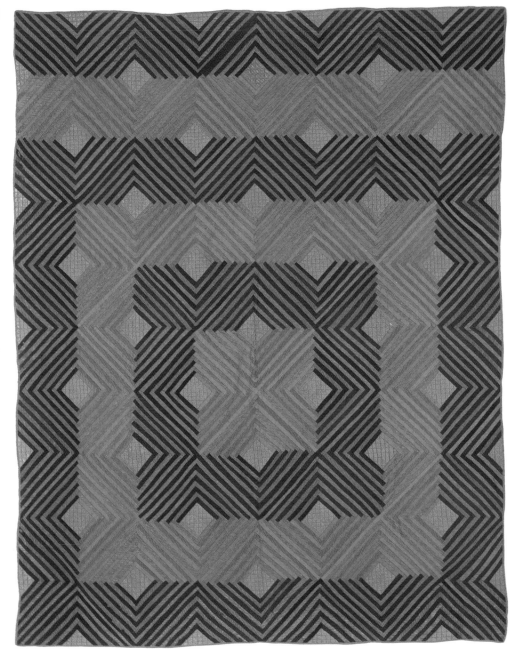

Organized by The Kentucky Quilt Project 1800–1900, Inc., in cooperation with the Museum of History and Science, Louisville, Kentucky, and the Smithsonian Institution Traveling Exhibition Service, Washington, D.C.

Library of Congress Cataloging in Publication Data

Holstein, Jonathan.
    Kentucky quilts, 1800–1900.

    Reprint. Originally published: Louisville, Ky.: Kentucky Quilt Project, 1982.
    Bibliography: p.
    1. Quilts—Kentucky—History—19th century—Exhibitions.   I. Finley, John, 1938-   II. Kentucky Quilt Project.   III. Title.
NK9112.H622   1983   746.9'7'09769
074013   83-12102
ISBN 1-880584-03-4

Manufactured in the United States of America
3rd printing 1992
The Kentucky Quilt Project, Inc.

Acknowledgments

This Project was made available by a generous challenge grant from

HUMANA INC.

with matching funds provided by:
Anonymous
Bingham Enterprises Foundation of Kentucky, Inc.
Brown-Forman Distillers Corporation
Ann Finch
John R. Gaines
Glenmore Distilleries Company
Greater Louisville Fund for the Arts
Nancy Teed Hudlow
Kentucky Arts Council and The National Endowment
    for the Arts
Kentucky Department of the Arts
Liberty National Bank and Trust Company
Louisville Productions
Medley Distilling Company
Mr. and Mrs. Rowland Miller
George W. Norton Foundation
Philip Morris Incorporated
Mr. Charles Weisberg

Opening Festival Weekend, Louisville, Kentucky
    Sponsored by First National Bank of Louisville.

In Memoriam

Bruce Mann
March 1944–November 1980

Introduction

by Jonathan Holstein

Americans have been making and using quilts for over three centuries. The remarkable persistence of the craft indicates two things about quilts: their practicality and our sentimental attachment to them. Quilts are still useful to us, and so are still made. But the survival of the American patchwork quilt has equally as much to do with our hearts: no other thing Americans have made has been so universally loved.

Americans have taken justifiable pride in the utilitarian things they made that broke with European precedents and created new standards of efficiency and beauty: the steel ax and plow, the clipper ship, the swan's-neck sleigh. Our decorative arts have been equally cherished: the furniture of the Eastern seaboard, folk art of all kinds, glass, woven and sewn textiles. The American quilt most perfectly bridges the two types of objects in which Americans established new models: the superbly efficient things made for practical use whose beauty springs from design reduced to the most basic, efficient forms, and decorative objects using idioms developed in the New World. Quilts were at once the most efficient answer to a pressing need–warm bed coverings–and the best, in some cases the only, medium through which generations of American women could express their creativity.

The thought, care, and work that went into making a quilt insured it a secure place in American affections; Americans understood and respected such well-directed expenditures of energy. Too, textile working was an ancient embodiment of traditional feminine roles and virtues important to an agrarian society; there was notice and honor in making quilts. Thriftiness, the idea of making something of utility and beauty from scraps, was a part of this virtuous industry, less important in reality than in the mythology. The quilt's association with the bed, its sheltering of the important moments of life played out there, made particular quilts treasured family objects, as did the use in a quilt's construction of materials associated with family members. The quilting bee, one of a number of such labor-sharing social occasions in American rural life, took its own place in our image of our preindustrial Golden Age. For all of these reasons the quilt, as early as the late nineteenth century, had become what it

❀ *Plate 3. Rainbow. (Family's name for this design: Full and Change of the Moon.) Pieced quilt. Made by Ann Johnson Armstrong. Hickman County, Kentucky. Circa 1890. Cotton. 78" x 68". Collection of Margie Lynch.*

Variations of this design, a semicircle surmounted by sawteeth, are ancient favorites; New York Beauty and Crown of Thorns are others. They almost always work well visually. Here the maker designed and arranged the images to wonderful effect, creating a feeling of depth. Such illusion is quite rare in quilts. The quilt is somewhat slapdash (two ends were haphazardly worked out, the quilting is crude), but it is very successful as a visual creation.

remains–an internationally recognized symbol of American life and ideals.

The Industrial Revolution moved more and more Americans to the cities. Quiltmaking continued, however, especially in rural areas, through the first decades of the twentieth century. Then, perhaps spurred by the Depression, there was a more general revival of interest in the 1930s, and this occasioned the publication of some books on the subject that have become classics–the first simplified "how to" books, the first attempts at a systematic investigation of pattern types and derivations. These books are better on practical matters than history; much of the latter as presented was based more on supposition, ancestor worship, and nostalgia for an idealized past than on facts.

Recovery and World War II followed, and three decades during which no special note was taken of American quilts. Then, in the 1970s, a few pivotal museum exhibitions presented quilts as designed objects rather than American crafts. Many more exhibitions in museums devoted to the fine arts rather than crafts or folk art followed, both here and abroad. Books and articles that discussed quilts as art appeared, art collectors all over the world began to collect quilts to go up on walls with their paintings, and thus in a relatively short period of time quilts achieved a whole new status and celebrity; they became a new, distinct category of American folk art (they had not been that before) and art objects with international status.

This required some adjustments in thinking for Americans. The traditional criteria for judging excellence in quilts, in addition to overall beauty, were the craft aspects, the quality of stitching in the piecing or appliqueing, fineness and elaborateness of the quilting, the intricacy of the design, number of pieces used in the patterns, how well complicated maneuvers (sewing curves, making points meet, etc.) had been done. While quality of work remained a consideration, people who began to collect quilts as art were much more interested in the overall effect of the design, the balance of the colors–in the end, how well the quilt worked as a painting. A quilt of 10,000 pieces might be of much less interest, therefore, than a Lancaster County, Pennsylvania, Amish quilt with just a few huge elements. The reason for this quick celebrity was simple enough: many American quilts, especially pieced quilts, are amazing look-alikes for some modern paintings. Such images as those in the Baby Blocks variant (Plate 18) and the brilliant version of a Rainbow quilt type (Plate 3) are contemporary in feeling and would not be out of place in a museum devoted to the work of modern artists. Many such quilts were made a century or more before similar images appeared in nonobjective paintings.

One aspect of this was pure coincidence: the large format of quilts when hung flat against a wall rather than spread over a bed was similar to the size and format of many modern paintings. There was, of course, no direct link between the two mediums. I can find no instance before the 1970s when modern artists were directly influenced by quilt design. The women who made quilts were not by standard definition artists, they did not consider themselves such, were not primarily engaged in making art, and did not see themselves in an art-historical framework. They had little or no awareness of painting, modern or otherwise.

Other similarities occurred, however, because of a strange convergence of intent. The American quiltmaker was concerned with both beauty and efficiency; she

✳ *Plate 4. Bear's Paw or Duck's Foot in the Mud. Pieced quilt. Probably made by Virginia Stewart. Gracey, Kentucky. Circa 1899. Cotton. 87" x 72". Collection of The Kentucky Museum. Bowling Green, Kentucky. Record number 81.65.*

This is a bold use of this pattern, the colors and proportions such that the images seem almost too small for their frames. The maker decided to separate the blocks with interior borders popularly called "sashes," and she added a bit of life to those with miniature nine-patch blocks, an unusual feature. Compare the results here to another quilt using the same pattern, Plate 5. The fading observable here is almost always seen in that blue-green material. It seems to have been colored with particularly unstable, or difficult to mordant, dyes, which fade to a greenish-brown.

developed a work method that was suited to American conditions–the block style. This style developed from border elements of earlier high-style English and American quilts–squares that repeated a single geometric element. The American woman, faced with the necessity of producing many warm bedcovers in the most efficient manner possible, and wanting some design in them, developed the work method of using a single geometric image or geometricized representational image repeated in rows to cover the whole surface of a quilt. The blocks were joined either directly to each other (as seen in the Star quilt, Plate 39) or spaced with inner borders (as seen in the Bear's Paw quilt, Plate 4).

This method was used both for pieced and appliqué quilts. The advantages were many. The blocks could be individually lap-worked and one did not have to deal with an ever larger textile as work progressed. All the parts for a quilt top could be cut at once, with or without templates,

fig. 3. Martha Jane Riffe was posed by a traveling photographer, circa 1870, in front of a tapestry which he hung in her home. She made the "Dove at the Window" quilt. Plate 5.

insuring identical blocks whose parts would mesh if the quilt design used linking blocks. The adoption of this method meant a move away from the busier, more crowded quilts in the English and American high style popular at the turn of the nineteenth century. The tops of such quilts were built mosaic fashion, each element added to the work that had gone before. The style survives in such quilts as the Baby Blocks quilt (Plate 17) and the Star quilt. (Plate 12)

As was true of many other things that began on this continent as copies of European prototypes, distinctly American versions reflecting changed attitudes and conditions quickly appeared. Many objects, such as the steel plow and ax, broke completely with their precursors; other things–furniture, pottery, quilts–moved toward a more simplified, open statement. There are good English precedents for the single large star image on a quilt, but no English quilt would have used it in the direct and simple manner seen in the Star quilt (Plate 13). Nor would an English maker have set single images in white fields as in

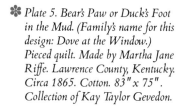 Plate 5. Bear's Paw or Duck's Foot in the Mud. (Family's name for this design: Dove at the Window.) Pieced quilt. Made by Martha Jane Riffe. Lawrence County, Kentucky. Circa 1865. Cotton. 83" x 75". Collection of Kay Taylor Gevedon.

This pattern is one of many drawn from the unspoiled natural world which surrounded and so impressed earlier Americans. Its limited use of color and carefully proportioned elements indicate the maker's wish to create a restrained and elegant quilt; in that she was successful. Her temperament is further revealed in the unhurried, very fine stitches and the simple, ordered lines of quilting. It is interesting to compare this quilt visually to another of the same pattern, Plate 4, to see how the same design could be manipulated for totally different results. It is clear that succeeding generations cherished the quilt; its yellow, green and brown, early aniline colors quite prone to fading, are as bright as new, indicating the quilt was little, if at all, exposed to light.

the elegant Rising Sun quilt (Plate 47). This movement to a distinctly American visual idiom was largely completed by the mid-nineteenth century, the new ideas developing enormously thereafter.

There grew a body of quilt design based, for reasons of efficient production and ease of visual manipulation, on geometric divisons of the square, in which both representational and nonrepresentational images were used. The Flower Basket quilt (Plate 9), in which the essential elements needed to visually identify such an object have been distilled, is an example of the former type of image; the Star quilt (Plate 32) represents the latter.

The development of aniline dyes in the mid-nineteenth century brought to quiltmakers a greatly expanded range of colors in cottons and wools, and the ever-increasing efficiency of cotton processing and weaving made a greater variety of materials available at lower costs. This brought about a great flowering of quilt design in the second half of the nineteenth century, particularly in the last quarter.

An ocean away, the seeds of modern art had been well planted and were beginning to flower. In the extraordinary artistic turmoil of the early twentieth century were seen both the beginnings of nonrepresentational art and a conscious movement to geometric forms as a basis for both painting and sculpture. The Bauhaus taught many emerging artists who were to be pivotal in modern art history the possibilities inherent in unadorned geometry, and such artists as Mondrian and Albers used simple forms to express complex ideas and emotions.

This was, perhaps, the great discovery of twentieth-century art–that complex ideas and feeling could be evoked in painting and sculpture without reference to representational images. And it so happened that many of the visual solutions such artists, and artists who came after them, reached were similar to the solutions to aesthetic problems found by quiltmakers. Both artists and quiltmakers reduced common objects to their basic forms, the still lifes of the cubists and the Flower Basket quilt (Plate 9), for instance. Both employed a single format in many color and scale variations, as in the Homage to the Square paintings of Josef Albers and Lancaster Amish Diamond quilts; in both cases, the sizes of component parts and the colors of a largely set format were varied to achieve different results. Both explored color and tone possibilities in a systematic manner, as seen in the work of such painters as Max Bill and the Lancaster Amish Sunshine and Shadow quilts or those such as the Baby Block quilt. (Plate 17.) The explosive imagery of the Prairie Star quilts (Plate 13) found echoes in the imagery of such pop painters as Roy Lichtenstein, as did the use of serial images in the work of

✽ *Plate 6. Detail of plate 7.*

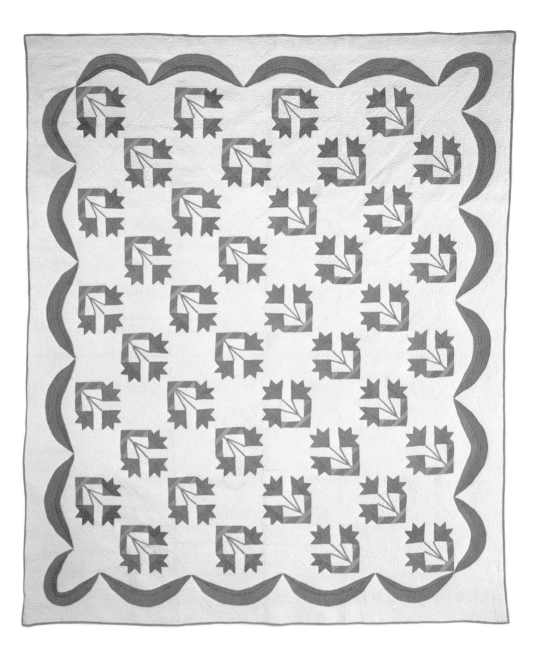

✽ Plate 7. North Carolina Lily.
Pieced and appliqué quilt. Made by
a female member of the Hart family. Clark County, Kentucky. Circa
1865. Cotton. 97" x 81". Collection of Sarah Scobee (Mrs. Hugh
B.) Hammet.

The pattern is a very early one–
basically half of the Star of
Lemoyne design with an added tri-
angle to form the base of each
flower. It is almost always used as a
group of three with some finishing
elements at the base of the stems to
fill out the square, the intended
effect a naturally growing cluster.
The stems are often, as here, appliquéd. The gracefully looped swag
border is a nice counterpoise to the
rigidity of the flowers.

The overall composition of this
quilt is a marvel. Quilts with representational images can be arranged
in several ways. All images can run
one way (as in the Baskets quilt,

Plate 9,) so that there is a definite
top and bottom, or the field can be
split along one axis, diagonal,
length or widthwise, and the blocks
arranged so that whichever end is
used at the head, half of the images
will read right side up, half reversed.
This quilt's maker chose the latter
course but made the border swag
design symmetrical along a diagonal
axis while the fields of lilies are
symmetrical–that is, half standing
one way, half the other–along a
midline lengthwise axis, and they
are slanted. The way in which the
border and the field interrelate is
worth some study; their symmetrical
axis is at the midpoint widthwise.

These careful arrangements do
make the quilt read well with either
end as the head. But their real purpose was to conceal a private gesture: at one end one of the blocks is
reversed. There has been much men-
tion of such intentional irregulari-
ties, the notion being that, since

only God can make perfect things,
human beings should not attempt to
emulate His perfection, and a pur-
poseful mistake in an otherwise perfect thing is a sign of devotion. I have,
however, seen only a very few quilts
in which I believed there were intentional, designed anomalies; most, on
analysis, turn out to be due to care-
lessness, lack of proper materials to
finish all the blocks the same way,
etc. In this quilt, as in the few others
I have seen with such a gesture,
great effort has been made to conceal rather than emphasize it. I have
seen them mostly in quilts that
required very careful planning and
that were of superb workmanship,
and in which the irregularity
required such elaborate manipula-
tions to make the quilt work visually that there could be no mistaking
the intent. Whether such manipula-
tions of design were to honor God's
perfection or were an expert quiltmaker's private visual joke, I do

not know. She has also hidden in the
quilting along one edge five family
names and a date. One name, E. J.
Hart, is also quilted into another
Hart family quilt. (Plate 23.) She
was likely the maker of both. It, too,
has an unmistakable intentional
mistake.

such artists as Andy Warhol. Many more such similarities can be seen and have been noted and appreciated by those interested in the arts; it has encouraged the collecting of quilts by those who also collect modern paintings. Such collectors have normally been drawn to bold geometric quilts with straight-cut designs.

At the same time, the many exhibitions, articles, and books on quilts that have appeared since the early seventies have introduced them to many whose interest in art is not confined to the modern. They may, in fact, see and cherish in quilts the traditional values so long associated with them. Such appliqué quilts as the Rose of Sharon quilt (Plate 25) and the Rose quilt (Plate 38) are desirable to collectors precisely because they have such unmistakable American images, simplified and charming, with strong visual elements.

Because of the enormous growth of interest in the subject, quilt mini-industries have been hatched: schools of quilt design and technique, specialized fabric and equipment suppliers, publications, workshops, seminars. In addition to the many making quilts in traditional patterns, there are gifted amateur and professional quiltmakers who are creating new visual idioms for the craft. Some base their designs on traditional forms used in new ways, with new color sensibilities. Others are creating entirely new forms and types of designs. In either case there is the wonderful feeling of working in a continuum of design and thoughtful craftsmanship that stretches unbroken to American beginnings.

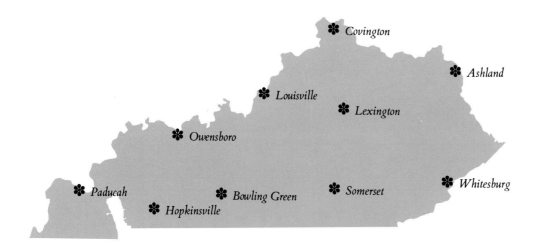

Quilt Day Locations

Preface

by John Finley

❊ *Plate 8. New York Beauty. Pieced quilt. Kentucky. Circa 1875. Cotton. 86" x 73". Private collection.*

This is a version of a pattern that always makes a visually interesting quilt. Usually the rays of the semicircles and the thin fingers of the bars between them end in sharp points, giving the quilts a vaguely menacing quality, as if they were fields of cactus. The result here is no less effective for the lack of points; the quilt looks like a section of intricate machinery of some sort–watch works or gear trains. The pattern in any variation is laborious to make, so it was usually used for best pieced quilts. Often the pattern is accompanied by extra-good quilting, and here it is lavish, the entire surface carefully treated, curved feathers outlining the semicircles, and in the middle of each small sunburst that centers the white squares where the sashes cross, there is a heart. Hearts often appear in better quilts. It has been said that such hearts were put into quilts made by engaged girls to go with them for the wedding bed, and no doubt some were so used. But I think more often they were put into quilts simply because they were ancient and beloved signs of affection and it was pleasant to think of them hidden in a quilt covering a loved one.

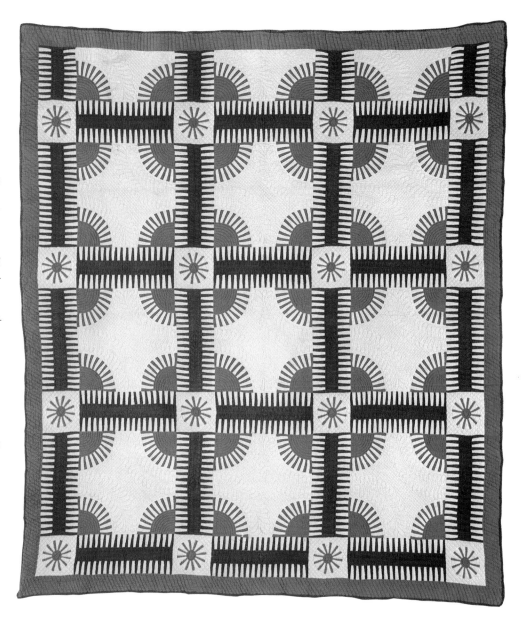

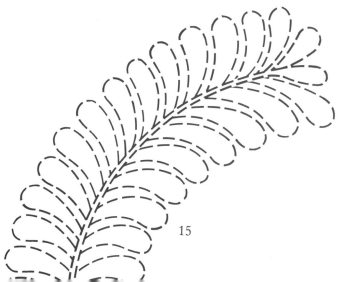

In *Women in Kentucky,* Helen Deiss Irvin writes that women settlers were migrating to Kentucky–to stay– as early as 1775, yet "they are usually ignored in histories, as if they were invisible or their lives of little interest."

Whether invisible or ignored, countless women left their marks on Kentucky's heritage, many of them through their rich legacy of needlework, a legacy that Bruce Mann recognized and admired. A Louisville quilt dealer, Mann had sold a number of nineteenth-century quilts to out-of-state collectors when he realized the quilts were a part of Kentucky's artistic heritage. These old quilts

15

could vanish, he foresaw, before Kentuckians had a chance to know them or appreciate their value.

"As time passes," he wrote, "quilts deteriorate, are lost through negligence or catastrophe, or merely leave the state, depriving us of the privilege of their company."

Mann had an idea for a project to preserve "for posterity what still remains of our early quilt heritage," and he viewed that heritage as considerable:

"Kentucky is a fascinating crossroads, the first state settled west of the Alleghenies. Its settlement neatly straddled the Industrial Revolution, and it was far enough removed from the European-dominated sophistication of the original colonies to develop its own unique forms. It was a fertile area for early quilt-making, two of the most important quilts known (the Russellville fair and the Graveyard quilts) having originated here."

Mann proposed a three-part project. First, important early Kentucky quilts would be located and documented.

Second, the best of these would be collected for a major museum exhibition. Third, a book would be written about the quilts and what they could reveal about the nineteenth century. He wrote:

"The textile industry was the cutting edge of the Industrial Revolution, which changed us from a landed society to a modern manufacturing community. Quilts are the perfect documentary of this upheaval, containing within their brightly colored patches a history and encyclopedum of textile evolution...

With rare exception, quilts were made by women, and as such provide nearly the only record left by presuffrage housewives and pioneers. A great deal can be deduced about their makers from the evidence incorporated in the design organization, fabric selection, workmanship, etc...."

In 1980, before he could get the project launched, Mann was killed in a traffic accident. Two of his friends, Eleanor Bingham Miller and Shelly Zegart, decided to carry on with his proposal. Joined by Eunice Ray and Katy Christopherson, they started The Kentucky Quilt Project: 1800-1900.

Their immediate problem was to find the quilts. Somehow they would have to get the word around all of Kentucky's 120 counties that they were interested in nineteenth century Kentucky quilts. They would have to get people to dig through their attics and cedar chests and bring their quilts somewhere to be examined and documented.

Ms. Ray developed the idea of the Quilt Days. Rather than expect the quilt owners to come to The Kentucky Quilt Project, she proposed taking The Kentucky Quilt Project to the people and giving them an incentive to show their quilts.

Twelve Quilt Days were held, between July 1981 and March 1982, in Bowling Green, Somerset, Louisville, Lexington, Owensboro, Hopkinsville, Ashland, Paducah, Whitesburg, and Covington, with two in Somerset and in Louisville.

Mrs. Christopherson, with her links to the Kentucky Heritage Quilt Society, arranged for volunteers from local quilting groups and, where possible, museums. In advance of the Quilt Days, posters were put up and local women's groups or quilting circles were contacted. There were ads in the local newspapers and feature stories, and the news also spread by word of mouth.

As an incentive, The Kentucky Quilt Project offered a $100 prize for the best nineteenth century quilt documented at each of the Quilt Days, and the project directors put together a program they thought the quilt owners would enjoy.

❉ *Plate 10. Star. Pieced quilt. Made by Robert Toupe. Maysville, Kentucky. Circa 1876. Cotton. 79" x 79". Collection of Betty Horton.*

While similar in conception and scale to the Star quilt in Plate 13, this quilt uses an even simpler palette, only three colors, lines shooting from the center, and small surrounding stars the same size and color as the center of the main image. Repetition of the image in different scale was a common device in these large Star quilts from their inception. This is about as reduced as the format became, and it is interesting to compare it to an earlier version of the same idea, the Star quilt in Plate 12, to see how American quiltmakers simplified images for visual effect. The quilt was evidently made by a man, Robert Toupe, a harness maker, and family history states he sewed it while he was convalescing from an injury. A few other quilts we have seen that were made by men were produced during such periods of enforced inactivity.

There was interest in the prize money, to be sure, but it turned out that the project directors had greatly underestimated the quilt owners' enthusiasm for the project and their hunger for information.

"People have these quilts and they know they have value in them," Ms. Miller said, "but they really don't know what they've got in terms of heritage and monetary value."

They went to the Quilt Days to find out. Carrying plastic bags bulging with quilts, they turned out in greater numbers than anyone had expected. Usually they were women; sometimes they were men. Often they were in their retirement years–keepers of the family histories as well as keepers of the family quilts. And while one could sense a keen edge of competition among them, the atmosphere of the typical Quilt Day was festive. There was great family pride in these quilts; this was a place to share it with a community of friends and neighbors.

As the quilt owners arrived, the local volunteers took them in hand. Mrs. Christopherson, with her academic knowledge of quilts and firsthand experience at quilting, helped identify patterns and other physical characteristics

18

of the quilts. Ms. Miller talked to the owners about the history of the quilts and about the quiltmakers, making notes for the project's records.

As the day was getting organized and the quilt owners settled down to waiting for their own quilt, or quilts, to be examined, Ms. Zegart showed a film about quilting and told the visitors about the Project.

Each of the quilts had to be unfolded and carefully arranged for photographing, and Ms. Zegart used these moments to critique the quilts, while the owners gathered around and listened. But she also gave them a more general talk, describing how to recognize value in old quilts and how to care for them. Even though she is a quilt dealer, she urged the quilt owners not to sell their quilts. Make every effort to keep the quilts within your own family, she told them, and if you can't keep them in the family, donate them to a museum that will keep them well–The Kentucky Museum in Bowling Green or The Kentucky History Museum located at The Kentucky Historical Society in Frankfort.

"Preserve Kentucky's quilt heritage," was the message driven home during each of the Quilt Days.

When they had ended, upwards of 1,000 quilts had

❋ *Plate 11. Star. Pieced quilt with appliqué three-dimensional floral bouquets. Made by Fannie Sales Trabue. Todd County, Kentucky. Circa 1860. Silk and velvet. 70" x 70". Collection of Sara Lee Trabue Lacy.*

This Star quilt is transitional in form between the distinctly high-style quilt (Plate 12), and the two later, very American versions (Plate numbers 10 and 13). It retains an outer border (worked with diamond-formed triangles), and decorated corners, often rendered in a high-style Star quilt in floral chintz appliqués. The many colors used in the star is also typical of the earlier type. It is very "refined," considered a desirable attribute at the time it was made.

been examined and documented and several encouraging conclusions had been reached. The project directors had feared that many of Kentucky's better quilts might already have left the state, but this appeared not to be the case. Also, it was evident that the Quilt Days had not nearly exhausted Kentucky's quilt resources.

Further, the Quilt Days gave credence to Mann's conviction that the project "would go a long way toward demonstrating the elegance of early Kentucky decorative arts" and would dispel the image of the Kentucky quilt as being a "chenille bedspread from Appalachia."

Another important lesson of the project was not just that valuable heirlooms can be lost, worn out, or sold away, but that important elements of family history can vanish within a generation. Because quilt making is largely an anonymous art, the identity of the quiltmaker usually could not be determined; most often, there simply was no information that would cast any light on her life and times. In most cases, no family stories survived to suggest that even such historic and massive upheavals as the Civil War touched their lives.

In appraising the findings of The Kentucky Quilt Project, Mrs. Christopherson said that "the threads are thin" even when it comes to assigning a given quilt to a given quiltmaker. She wrote:

"Many whys remained unanswered, as do many whats. Think of quilts, treasured and kept or sold, in either case, no trace of the maker may remain. Fabrics–did they come from Europe? The ball gowns of the family? Purchased as remnants from New York's fancy dress houses? Which peddlers brought which goods and by what route? The quiltmaker: Rich? Poor? What ethnic background?

While the quilts are links to just such information, today little can be proved. We are one generation if not two too late to find all the stories which were passed on by word of mouth in the long winter evenings."

The quilts in this book for which family history could be unearthed have double value: they are both visual and historical documents which give us concrete links to our past. Months after the Quilt Days had ended, project coordinator Dorothy West crisscrossed the state to pick up the quilts that would be in the exhibition and found that an interest in genealogy had been awakened in many of the quilt owners.

The quilts are keyholes through which to glimpse a partial picture of Kentucky history. The lives of the quiltmakers bring color and movement to these fleeting views.

Kentucky Quilts

❋ Plate 12. Star. (Family's name for this design: Star of Bethlehem.) Pieced quilt. Kentucky. Circa 1840. Cotton. 117" x 114". Collection of Waveland State Shrine, Lexington, Kentucky.

A classic high-style Star quilt, the type can be found as early as the late eighteenth century both here and in England and is still, with little change, being made. This has many features one would expect to find in such a quilt–the large size, the immense central image with echoing stars in the corners and on the sides, the Wild Goose Chase border, and the use of better materials–chintzes and fine cottons. Such quilts were made for the important bed or beds in a comfortable house–larger than later beds. The beautiful colors are typical of pre-aniline dyes.

As the eighteenth century drew to a close, Kentucky was rapidly losing all vestiges of frontier society. Organized Indian raids had ceased with the Battle of Blue Licks, one of the last armed conflicts of the American Revolutionary War. This battle, fought in Kentucky, brought together all of the elements of frontier strife–the wilderness, the Indians, the settlers, the British, even that famed symbol of the American frontier, Daniel Boone. Up to a point, the action followed the pattern of the typical frontier Indian fight: the Indians would raid Kentucky farms or settlements from their lands north of the Ohio. The frontiersmen would band together to retaliate. Sometimes the settlers would catch the raiding parties, exchange shots, and inflict some punishment; usually they would succeed only in chasing the Indians back out of the territory.

On August 18, 1782, a force of 182 Kentucky men set out to pursue a group of British-led Indians who had been raiding homes and settlements in central Kentucky. The Indians were heading north, ostensibly fleeing back to their tribal lands. On the morning of August 19, on a bend of the Licking River, the Kentuckians spotted some of the Indians, apparently in full retreat. After a brief council, the settlers plunged headlong into the chase. Unfortunately, they had fallen into a well-planned ambush. More than a third of the Kentuckians were killed or captured. Boone lost a son and historian Steven A. Channing wrote that "some of the brightest pioneer settlement leaders" were among those who died.

This brutal frontier engagement was only ten years in the past when Kentucky became the newest state in the Union–the fifteenth–with a population of more than 70,000 persons. In 1800 the census showed that the population had increased to 179,873 whites, 739 "free colored," and 40,343 slaves, and by 1810 these numbers had jumped to 324,237 whites, 1,713 free blacks, and 80,561 slaves.

In *A History of Kentucky* Thomas D. Clark writes that this "wholesale immigration" was due, in part, to "a popularization of the frontier, coupled with a scarcity of good land available to immigrants along the east coast." Another factor adding to the western movement was Virginia's use of frontier land to pay off its Revolutionary soldiers. At the same time, many Tories were moving westward to escape the ill feelings and mistreatment of the postwar period.

In *Kentucky* Channing writes that geography gave Kentucky "a fateful position" for migration: "The rivers of the eastern states flowed to the Atlantic; Kentucky's pointed westward, toward the interior, toward the Mississippi. The region was also centrally located, jutting into the west like some great arrow. Over the coming decades, the commonwealth became a major conduit for thousands who would eventually move on, they or their children, into the northwest and southwestern states."

The Ohio River was the natural route for the westward-bound families of the Middle Atlantic states. By 1815 there were steamboats on the river. More than 400 of them passed through the Portland Canal at Louisville in 1831, the first year the canal was open, and in 1845 this number was up to 1,585. The flatboats and keelboats, which had predated steamboats, continued to add to the traffic.

Settlers migrating from North Carolina and southern Virginia funneled through the Cumberland Gap, fanning out across Kentucky and Tennessee over the old trails of

fig. 4. *Judy Ann Scott, creator of the Prairie Star quilt, posed for this portrait, circa 1900, with her daughter, Joe Ann. Plate 13.*

Plate 13. Prairie Star. Pieced quilt. Made by Judy Ann Scott. Temple Hill, Kentucky. Circa 1880. Cotton. 83" x 72". Collection of Dickey Wilkinson Parker.

This pattern is also known as Harvest Sun in the Midwest, Ship's Wheel in New England, and Star of Bethlehem in Pennsylvania. It has always been a popular pattern, used, as its many names would indicate, in all parts of the country. Making the many diamond points meet correctly is not a job for a novice seamstress. This quilt uses a restrained palette–three basic colors for the star, subdued green and brown for the border–very effectively. It is at once somber and intense. Strong arrowlike rays in the border colors shoot into the star from the sides, a device that intensifies the drama of the central image.

the buffalo and the Indians. Several major trails led into the heart of Kentucky–the Bluegrass region–and pioneer families like the Estills followed these, staking out farms in the fertile, rolling countryside.

Samuel Estill was born on the family farm in central Kentucky and his daughter Amanda was born there in 1810. The family history gives Estill the title of general, possibly self-bestowed and probably from service as an Indian fighter.

The days of fighting Indians were all but forgotten, and central Kentucky was well into an antebellum period of gentleman farming when, in 1831, Amanda was married to Franklin Moran. He owned an 880-acre farm in the Bluegrass region with a large white frame house and slaves. (Plate 14.)

Kentucky had few large plantations, according to Channing, but its agricultural economy was dominated by slaveholders. Only 2 percent of the rural population

Plate 14. Pineapple, Rose of Sharon, and Pink (?). Appliqué quilt. Made by Amanda Estill Moran. Garrard County, Kentucky. Circa 1860. Cotton. 100″ x 86″. Collection of Mrs. John Wade Walker.

This exuberant creation manages to stop just this side of disorder. While packed with images, it still works as a whole. There are pineapples in two forms, the smaller connected to Rose of Sharons, the larger to a flower that might be a Pink. Such botanical impossibilities are common in American folk art, particularly in the work of the Pennsylvania Germans and in such appliqué quilts. This is not a mathematically precise quilt. Some images reach a little too far, almost touching others, some leaves touch the edges, others in complimentary images do not, etc. Yet its joyous quality overcomes such lack of perfection in the manner of much good folk art.

❋ Plate 15. *Princess Feather with Oak Leaves. Appliqué and pieced quilt. Made by Mahulda Mize. Circa 1860. Cotton. 72" x 71". Collection of Mrs. Richard Cotton.*

The pristine condition of this quilt, especially the unfaded state of colors particularly susceptible to light, indicates careful preservation in the family of its maker. The pattern was derived from the Prince of Wales' feathered insignia, the prince's feathers changed to Princess Feather in the New World. Often the design was, as here, combined with oak leaves. This is a particularly lively version of the pattern, the delicate border emphasizing the boldness of the feather clusters. The overlapping at the base of the feathers to give the design some depth is a nice touch, as are the circles added like bells to the end of each stalk.

owned ten slaves or more, yet this 2 percent owned a majority of all slaves, possessed more improved acreage, and produced more of the farm products sold in 1860 than did all of the small nonslaveholding farmers put together.

In *Women in Kentucky,* Ms. Irvin writes that household service was more typical than field work for Kentucky slave women, and she cites the account of Susan Dale Sanders, whose father was a field worker:

"I used to carry tubs of clothes down to the old spring house, there was plenty of water, and I washed all the clothes there. I and my sisters used to wash and sing and we had a good time. Mammy worked hard, did all the cooking."

Mahulda Mize was a slave on an estate in Clay County, along the edge of the Bluegrass region. She did not pass along much to her descendants about her days in servitude nor the period just after she was set free. She did tell her family, however, that she finished making her Princess Feather quilt in 1850, when she was eighteen years old. No doubt the quilt was made for her owners, for a slave girl would not have had the money to buy such fabrics. It also is not likely that she would have been granted the

❀ *Plate 17. Baby Blocks. Pieced quilt. Made by Julia Wickliffe Beckham. Queensboro, Kentucky. Circa 1870. Silk and velvet. 86" x 82". Collection of Judge George V. Triplett.*

Julia Beckham's quilt, according to family history, is constructed of fabrics saved from gowns. Certainly such best-dress silks and velvets found their way into these high-style quilts, really meant more as elegant parlor or boudoir throws. The design is ancient, one of the few optical illusion designs used by American quiltmakers, and requires the placement in a coordinated manner of light, medium-tone, and dark-colored diamonds.

leisure and the freedom to create such a thing for her own use. (Plate 15.)

Sentiment ran strong against slavery among the mountain people, according to *The History of Clay County,* and a notable Clay County slaveholder, John Hyden, fled to his native Lee County, Virginia, when the Civil War broke out. The outbreak of the war also prompted a prominent Bardstown family, the Wickliffes, to leave their home temporarily and to seek haven in Canada.

By the time of the Civil War, the Wickliffes had a reputation for lavish Southern-style living. Charles A. Wickliffe was born in a pioneer homestead in central Kentucky, and he was a prosperous young lawyer with a promising career in politics when, in 1813, he built Wickland –the mansion that was to become known as "The Home of Governors."

Wickland was constructed on an 800-acre estate that had been a wedding gift to Wickliffe and his bride, the former Margaret Crepps, from her uncle, Dr. Walter Brashear, who was known for performing the first hip operation. Built of brick, the fourteen-room house stood three stories high. It had colonial-style double parlors and a wide spiral stairway to the third floor. Architect John Rogers of Baltimore was lavish in his use of windows. The many windows and the fourteen-foot ceilings gave Wickland a very bright and airy feeling.

Charles Wickliffe started his political career as a state representative and he eventually became governor of Kentucky. He and Margaret had eight children. Their son Robert, born at Wickland in 1819, moved to Louisiana for the warmer climate and became that state's last pre-Civil War governor.

Only one of the children, Julia Tevis Wickliffe, continued to live on the family estate after reaching adulthood. She married a lawyer, William Netherton Beckham, and he took over the management of the plantation while Julia managed Wickland and raised ten children. One of their sons, John Crepps Wickliffe Beckham, became the third governor of the family.

With their slaves at Wickland and their obvious family ties below the Mason–Dixon line, the Wickliffes were Confederate sympathizers, and at one point during the Civil War Julia and William Beckham took their children and fled Wickland to escape harassment.

Julia's quilt is made up of fabrics from family ball dresses and gowns–keepsakes of happy, easier times before the war. (Plate 17.)

While the richness of the Bluegrass region made it a goal for many early settlers who passed through the Cumberland Gap, others found their way from there to different parts of the state. The Peaks left Richmond, Virginia, sometime around 1850 with their four children, the youngest of whom, Isabella, was then about ten. (There were eventually to be twelve, six boys and six girls.) Their covered wagon contained, among other things, a loom and chests of equipment and materials for weaving, tatting, and sewing. As had the Estills, they traveled through the Gap, a one-time wilderness trail that was heavily traveled by the second decade of the nineteenth century; it earned the nickname of "Kaintuck Hog Road" because of all of the livestock that was driven over it, headed for markets east. When the Peaks reached the Tennessee River, however, they followed the river roads northwest, finally settling near where the Tennessee empties into the Ohio River in western Kentucky.

It was here that Isabella Peak met John Fleming. Born in Tennessee, Fleming had set out to make his living on the rivers, and he was a steamboat captain when they met. They married in the 1850s and he gave up the rivers for a farm on what was to become known as Fleming Hill, near Kuttawa. He also became a minister, establishing the first

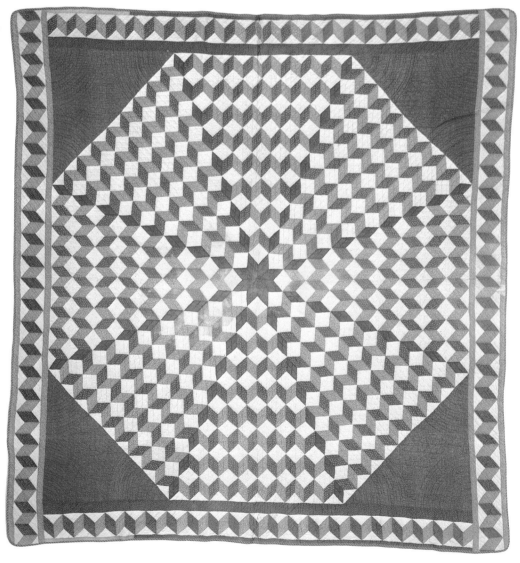

✽ Plate 18. Baby Blocks variant. (Family's name for this design: Lone Star.) Made by Isabella Fleming and Doris Boucher. Paducah, Kentucky. Circa 1885. Cotton. 81" x 81". Collection of Mrs. Kate Boucher Hammond.

The optical illusion Baby Blocks design has been used here in a most unusual and effective manner to create an octagon centered by a red star. Red diamonds have been worked into the boxes where appropriate to create rays of light shooting from the star, and the design has been beautifully manipulated at the borders to create stairs. The palette has been kept to a minimum–four colors– which always makes this design cleaner visually. The overall effect is harmonious and complex. One sees the three-dimensional quality of the borders and central image, and the star, and is also aware that it looks like a benign spider's web.

❋ Plate 19. Baby Blocks arranged in the form of a cross. Pieced quilt. Made by Margaret Younglove Calvert. Bowling Green, Kentucky. Circa 1870. Cotton, wool, silk, and mohair. 77" x 72". Collection of The Kentucky Museum. Bowling Green, Kentucky. Record number 4031.

The Baby Blocks design is used in this unique quilt as isolated design elements set on fields and as the defining structure for the central cross. The composition uses the optical-illusion effect of the blocks to create a surreal landscape in which the cross and the field behind work together or at different levels, the blue background a third element in this play of planes.

The color choices were tough and painterly ones. There was no attempt at elegant color matching; they are jarring and emphasize the brutality and vigor of the composition. Such large-scale painterly compositions are quite unusual in American quilts. The use of repeated images precluded grand gestures and design and color choices were often limited by accepted taste.

Methodist church in the area.

With the help of slaves, the Flemings farmed about 500 acres, growing corn, tobacco, and cotton, among other crops, and raising turkeys, horses, and other livestock. It was an exceptional farm in that it did very well without the geographical advantage of being situated in the fertile Bluegrass region. But Fleming was more than a farmer; he was a former steamboat captain who knew all about getting his crops and livestock to market.

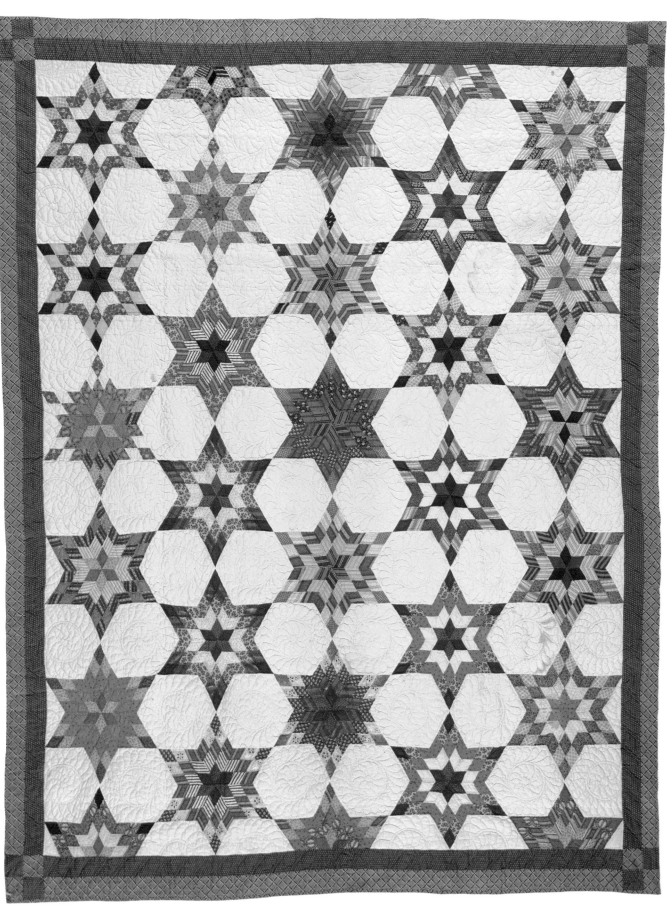

Plate 20. Ship's Wheel or Prairie Star variant. (Family's name for this design: Kentucky Star.) Pieced quilt. Made by Mary Sutherlin, her sister Nannie Elizabeth Pryor, and their sister-in-law Cora. Grave County, Kentucky. Circa 1865. Cotton. 84" x 66". Collection of Katherine Burton.

This popular pattern has had many names. Here a variant has been made with a six- rather than the more usual eight-pointed star. The star, in points from four up, was thoroughly explored as a design source by American quiltmakers. Star images were among the earliest and remained among the most popular quilt designs. They are satisfyingly dramatic visually and pleasing emotionally; Americans saw in them the Star of the Bible, the stars in their unspoiled night skies, the heavy suns of harvest time, images of a ship's compass, David's crown, the field of stars in their flag. It was an optimistic and exuberant image for a vigorous nation.

The quilt has a number of brown cottons popular for women's dresses; they are disintegrating, corroded by their dyes. The maker centered the design by positioning three blocks with dark materials around the central star along the quilt's midline. All of the other blocks use lighter materials around the center. The strong, simple borders compress the design, emphasizing its expansive quality.

fig. 5. A photograph of the family farm, circa 1900, shows Nannie Pryor Sutherlin with her husband, father, children and servants. She made the Kentucky Star quilt, with the help of a sister, Mary, and sister-in-law, Cora. Plate 20.

In *Agrarian Kentucky,* Thomas D. Clark writes that there were

"…two Kentuckys: one which produced a commercial surplus of crops and animals; another which lacked easy transportation access to markets.…

"While farmers on fertile Bluegrass soils measured growing wealth in crop surpluses which they shipped away to outside markets, subsistence farmers on poorer or more isolated lands were handicapped by lack of ready access to markets, varying qualities of soil, unevenness of topography and poor local leadership in all fields."

Because the Cumberland and Tennessee rivers slash across western Kentucky to join the Ohio and then the Mississippi, the Flemings enjoyed that important "ready access to markets" and the farm prospered.

There was a room known as the family room in the house on Fleming Hill. There Fleming women shared sewing tasks. The room had a stone fireplace with a large hearth, plenty of lamps, and big windows on the south and west sides. There was never a time of day when there wasn't good light for needlework, and the quilting frame was always in place.

In 1862 Isabella Fleming had given birth to Dora in the room with the quilting frame. John Fleming was gone at the time. He had freed his own slaves when the Civil War started and gone off to fight for the North, against members of his own family.

❃ *Plate 21. Detail of plate 22.*

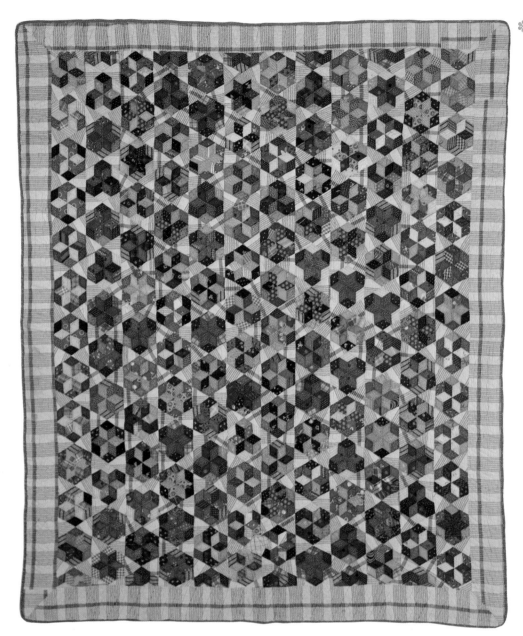

❋ *Plate 22. Hexagonal Star. Pieced quilt. Made by Mary Alexander. Cumberland County, Kentucky. Circa 1880. Cotton. 91" x 76½" Collection of Julia Neal.*

In this design a star pattern has been cleverly constructed of diamonds arranged in the light-midrange-dark sequence of material tonalities, which also creates the Baby Blocks design. The eye reads the design first one way, then another, the flat star, then the three-dimensional Block. Such dual-image blocks are quite rare in quilts, though some of the earliest pieced quilts have them, and this is perhaps due to the appearance of such images anciently in other mediums. In this quilt the hexagon enclosing the star also becomes the center of a larger six-pointed star, the arms composed of the light triangles which fill the spaces between the hexagons. The cotton materials are those that would have been used for shirts and wash dresses.

As April of 1862 began, Dora was two months old, and Isabella received word that John Fleming and his troops were rowing across the Ohio River at Smithland. They planned to camp along the road from Smithland to Dover, Tennessee, and then they were to march farther south to meet up with other Union forces.

Isabella did not hesitate. She bundled up the infant, mounted a horse, and, together with a former slave girl who had stayed on as a servant, rode off to intercept the column of troops. They found the soldiers that night, camped near the Gum Springs Baptist Church. There, while the men held a prayer meeting, Captain John Fleming was reunited with Isabella and introduced to his daughter, Dora.

The next day he rode off to the Battle of Shiloh. The commander of the Confederate forces in the battle was Albert Sidney Johnston. He was the most famous Kentuckian to die in the battle, which Channing sees as being "classic in posing Kentucky men and officers against one another." (Plate 18.)

Nearly 20,000 men died at Shiloh, the second major defeat for the South in the series of battles that made up the so-called Western Campaigns of 1862. The series ended with the Battle of Perryville, Kentucky, on October 8, 1862. Nearly 9,000 men died in the battle, which is counted as a Union victory because the Southern forces withdrew into Tennessee. Except for several more Confederate raids led by Kentucky native John Hunt Morgan, Perryville marked the virtual end of military actions in Kentucky. The South's hold on the river systems in western Kentucky was broken, and the Confederacy was never again able to mount a serious threat to Union dominance of the area.

❄ *Plate 23. Coxcomb with a Rose border. Pieced and appliqué quilt. Made by a female member of the Hart family. Clark County, Kentucky. Circa 1860. Cotton. 97" x 90". Collection of Sarah Scobee (Mrs. Hugh B.) Hammet.*

The central crosses are pieced and the flowers appliquéd in this unusual and very effective design. The highly stylized and aggressive central images and the naturalistic and restrained border are an unusual combination that might not have worked at all but manages to do so very well indeed–a testament to the maker's eye. While most of the very fine quilting is basically a grid, some follows the contours of the leaves and flowers and accentuates the design. This was commonly done on appliqué quilts. The quilt is signed in the quilting–E. J. Hart, as is another probably by the same hand, Plate 7. Though different visually, they are similar conceptually, innovative in design and masterful in the same way in balance and control. Most important, each has a great rarity, an intentional mistake. I will leave it to the reader to find it.

Strategists of both the South and the North had seen that Kentucky could tip the balance of power. It had men for their armies and resources to keep them fed and fighting. Geographically, it dominated the lower Ohio valley and offered potential control of the major western waterways. And while Kentucky had adopted a neutral posture, both sides saw the commonwealth as ripe for the picking. Channing wrote:

"More striking than citizens of any other state, Kentuckians appeared politically enigmatic, Southern in culture, militantly hostile to the death of the Union. Both sides appealed to them, both sides desperately needed them, but Kentuckians, seeking their own way, held back. Lacking the black majorities that excited deep racial fears farther south, lacking a militant band of younger slaveholders determined on expanding their fortunes, unwilling to abandon a tradition of devotion to the Union, realistic about the certainty of armed conflict, Kentucky held back."

When open fighting broke out, both the Confederate and Union armies ignored Kentucky's neutrality, quickly establishing bases inside the state along the Ohio and Mississippi rivers and elsewhere. General Johnston invaded his native state from Tennessee in the fall of 1861, establishing a headquarters at Bowling Green, in the south–central part of the state.

About forty miles to the west of Bowling Green was the birthplace of Jefferson Davis, the president of the Confederacy; about fifty miles to the northeast was the birthplace of Abraham Lincoln, president of the Union.

There was a colony of Shakers near Bowling Green, and they later wrote to President Lincoln:

"The armies of the South like a great Prairie fire swept over this part of Ky. in the fall & winter of 1861, licking up the substance of the land....They encamped for days as many as a thousand at a time, in our lots, and occupied our buildings. We chopped & halved wood for their camp fires & slaughtered our animals for their commissariat–and at all hours of the night, were we compelled to furnish diets for hundreds at a time."

✿ Plate 25. Rose of Sharon. Appliqué quilt with stuffed work and embroidery. Made by Cirendilla Allcock. Drake's Creek, near Bowling Green, Kentucky. Circa 1860. Cotton. 77″ x 103″. Collection of Novice Madison Robinson.

Such superb quilts were often made to celebrate a girl's coming of age, much as an apprentice would make a fine object to demonstrate the skills he had acquired and his readiness for journeyman's status. Needlework skills were essential to a wife in Cirendilla's time, and such quilts showed a young lady was ready for mature responsibilities. This is an almost perfect example of an American appliqué quilt with a pattern based on the popular Rose of Sharon motif, beloved because of its Biblical connotations. It has an extremely successful and imaginative border and superb quilting employing stuffed work to create sprays of different flowers, perfectly realized, and very dense background quilting to accentuate them. The quilt appears to have been made with a definite edge to head the bed (the edge with no border), an unusual feature.

✿ Plate 26. Detail of plate 25.

In 1861 Cirendilla Allcock and her two sisters each made a quilt for their hope chests, but it was an unsettled time even on their farm by the mill on Drake's Creek, east of Bowling Green. When the Allcocks heard that soldiers were coming, Cirendilla's mother hid the silver and other valuables under the bluff. The troops camped on the farm that night. They took the Allcocks' horses and killed some hogs. The quilts, including Cirendilla's Rose of Sharon, were spared. (Plate 25.)

🌸 *Plate 27. Detail of plate 28:*

Horses were a natural target of the foraging troops, but quilts also were a prized bit of booty. They could cushion a man's sleep on the hard ground or shield him from a summer night's dew or a winter night's frost. A soldier could wrap breakable items in a quilt and stuff them in a knapsack for safekeeping. Or he could throw a couple of purloined chickens into the center of a quilt, bring the corners together, throw the whole thing over a shoulder, and march off in anticipation of a pleasant evening meal.

Union troops were the ones doing the foraging in the countryside around Mrs. M. E. Poyner's home near Paducah in western Kentucky. She finished her quilt just before the war broke out, and because of the quilt's painstakingly stuffed "berries" and unique appliqué, it's easy to see why Mrs. Poyner didn't want to see it carried off. She is said to have hidden the quilt whenever troops came around–in a sugar chest, one story goes. (Plate 28.)

Some surviving family histories do not identify the troops who were marauding and pillaging over the countryside because both sides were guilty of some looting. Many Kentuckians became victims, regardless of their sympathies. Blue and gray armies crisscrossed parts of the state, and uniformed raiding parties like Morgan's ranged almost at will. There also was the Home Guard, a militia operating within the state on behalf of the North, and the Partisans, who were Kentuckians fighting on behalf of the South. Guerrilla bands robbed and murdered on behalf of both sides, although their ultimate loyalty to anyone was questionable. Outright brigands took advantage of all of the confusion.

It was no wonder that many Kentuckians hid their valuables at the first hint that *any* troops were nearby, regardless of their loyalties and regardless of the identity of the armed men.

❀ *Plate 28. Oak Leaf variant. Appliqúe quilt with padded work. Made by Mrs. M. E. Poyner. Paducah, Kentucky. Circa 1860. Cotton. 86" x 74". Collection of Mr. Hardin Pettit.*

This is perhaps the most relaxed, the folkiest, of the formal appliqué quilts in the book. It is very idiosyncratic, the swags reduced to strangely meandering curves, peculiar lines of padded work berries, very loose drawing. The effect is quite charming and lighthearted. The combination of green and red for major design components was a very popular one for appliqué quilts during the period; the introduction of aniline dyes had made those colors available in cotton bolts at reasonable prices. The quilt has a very elegant edging seen on three other appliqué quilts in the group (Plates 14, 23 and 25), cording enclosed in red material and that bound by green, the most complex edge treatment I have seen in American quilts.

Ellen Smith Tooke Vanzant was born in Kentucky in 1860, the year that South Carolina seceded from the Union, and her father, Irvin W. Smith, lost almost everything in the war.

Smith farmed in western Kentucky. He was a self-trained veterinarian–a "horse doctor," in rural parlance–and he married well. His bride, Martha Jane Mitchell, came from Ferry Corner Farm, a veritable estate of about 1,000 acres along the Cumberland River. There had been a time when a steamboat would stop at the farm, once a year, bringing bolts of cloth and supplies from England. For one of her wedding presents Martha Jane's parents gave her a slave, Aunt Moll.

Aunt Moll became Ellen's nanny, and in the years to come Ellen would tell of crying–and of Aunt Moll crying, too–as the freed slave woman walked down the road at the end of the war, leaving Smith's farm.

Through much of the war, soldiers and guerrillas came and went through the Smith farm, taking horses and livestock and stealing the family's food. On one raid they slit open the featherbeds looking for money and valuables. Martha Jane died during the war years, leaving Ellen without a mother at age four.

fig. 6. Ellen Smith Tooke Vanzant on the right, was the maker of the Lone Star Quilt. This photograph, circa 1940, shows her and her daughter, Mattie Tooke Morris, on the steps of Mattie's home. Plate 29.

Plate 29. Log Cabin Star. (Family's name for this design: Lone Star.) Pieced quilt. Made by Ellen Smith Tooke Vanzant. Trigg County, Kentucky. Circa 1890–1900. Cotton. 80" x 76". Collection of Sammie K. Morris.

This design is normally made in a smaller block repeated a number of times on the surface of the quilt and was so used in another quilt made by Ellen Vanzant, Plate 30. As are all such star quilts, this one is constructed from diamonds, but here diamonds cut from a fabric that had first been assembled from strips, like the logs of a cabin. (This type of work was called "string quilting" in Kentucky.) This is a no-nonsense utilitarian quilt, made quite thick for warmth (unlike often thinner "best" quilts), and crudely quilted. While such coarse quilting may affect the aesthetics of the quilt, it in no way impairs its function. In fact, the more quilting, the less effective the quilt as an insulator. Overall, the image is striking and powerful, a star blazing against the dark blue of the heavens, the kind of image handled so effectively by American quiltmakers.

✼ *Plate 30. Log Cabin Star. Pieced quilt. Made by Ellen Smith Tooke Vanzant and her daughter Mattie Tooke Morris, Trigg County, Kentucky. Circa 1890-1900. Cotton 82" x 80". Collection of Sammie K. Morris.*

The Vanzant family evidently liked this pattern; the same Log Cabin Star appears in a second quilt made by Ellen Vanzant alone (Plate 29), but in that one the image was used as a single large star on a blue ground. The two are a nice illustration of the facility and freedom with which American quilt-makers manipulated design scale, *using an image sequentially in small scale along the surface of a quilt for one effect, blowing up a single block to cover the whole surface for another. Essentially the same blue was used as the background color in each case, though in the multi-image quilt the stars were first set in white blocks, which were in turn imbedded in the blue. The blocks, tipped sideways, cause the blue to run in zigzag lines. Technically, the blue would be considered sashes in this quilt; visually it functions as a background.*

When the war ended, all Smith had left was his land and his two daughters. Ellen was the older, and at age six she stood on a kitchen chair and helped with the family cooking. (Plates 29 and 30.)

Aunt Moll and other Kentucky slaves were not officially freed in the state until 1865. Some black men enlisted in the Union army, but many others were impressed into duty. Ms. Irvin writes that with their men at war, the black women suffered, too.

"During the war itself, black women journeyed in droves to Camp Nelson, where their husbands or sons were training as Union soldiers. The Union commander, Speed S. Fry, called this situation the "Nigger Woman Question." He expelled the women and had those who returned whipped. But the strength of family ties led more black women and children to Camp Nelson, where they settled in small huts they themselves put up near the camp. Living conditions were miserable, and most were penniless."

Ms. Irvin writes that by mid-July of 1865 5,000 Kentucky blacks had crossed the Ohio River at Louisville into Indiana. And by November anywhere from 10,000 to 20,000 Kentucky blacks had left the state for the North.

fig. 7. Mattie Tooke Morris, shown in this photograph dated 1899, worked with her mother on the Log Cabin Star quilt. Plate 30.

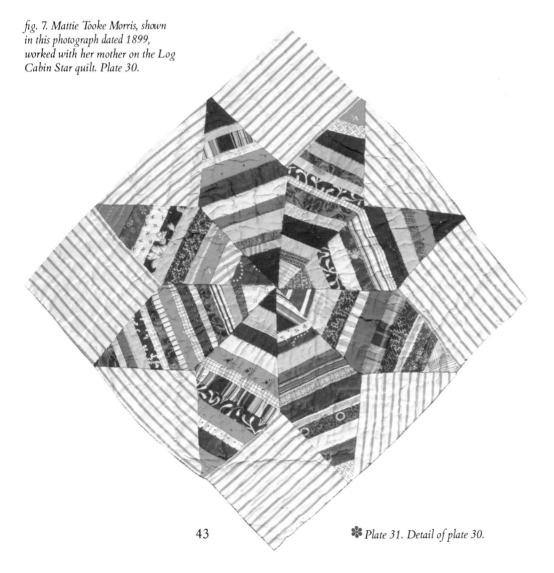

❁ *Plate 31. Detail of plate 30.*

The war devastated some Kentucky families. Yet, if the surviving family histories are any indication, the war seemed to swirl about the heads of other families without touching them. The only Civil War story passed down about Virginia Smith and John White Cooke, for example, seems to indicate that they were scarcely inconvenienced.

In Smiths Grove, not far from Bowling Green, Virginia and John were married on the day that Lincoln was inaugurated as President–March 4, 1861. Her quilt is made from the remnants of her trousseau, and the groom's velvet cravat is stitched into the center. The family story goes that the newlyweds set out on a honeymoon trip to Washington, but they turned back at Lexington on the advice that there was too much unrest for safe travel further east. (Plate 32.)

By contrast, the family of one of Virginia Smith's own daughters-in-law was virtually decimated on the male side. In a letter to Virginia the daughter-in-law gave an account of how the Civil War had affected her own father, John Kirtley, and his family.

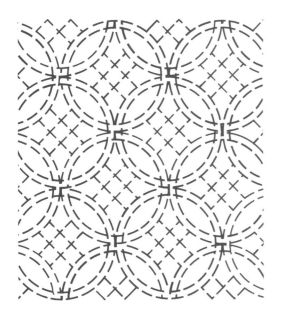

❀ *Plate 32. Star variation. Pieced quilt. Made by Virginia Bland Smith. Smiths Grove, Kentucky. Circa 1865–1870. Silk. 75½" x 68". Collection of Carolyn Cooke Makk and Dianne Cooke Jones.*

Quilts other than Crazy quilts can be used as family albums. According to family tradition, this quilt is in effect a wedding album of John and Virginia Smith, using pieces of their wedding-day finery. The father, undisputed head of the family, is at the center, represented by his wedding tie; all else radiates from him. Silk was the accepted luxury material of the day, and a woman's wardrobe would include at least one best silk dress if she could afford it. The quilt is in an ancient style (the central image built mosaic-style and enclosed with borders) in what was probably a conscious attempt to be elegant. The soft modulations of the silk colors are very effective in this design.

❀ Plate 33. Detail of plate 34.

❀ Plate 34. Penn's Treaty with the Indians. Whole-cloth quilt (made from three strips of the same fabric). Made by Sarah Runyan Anderson. Kentucky. Cloth late eighteenth century. Quilt early nineteenth century? Cotton. 93" x 93". Collection of the Kentucky Historical Society, Frankfort, Kentucky. Accession number 39.252.

French and English manufacturers were quick to offer citizens of the newly established republic fabrics printed with patriotic motifs, the hero Washington, William Penn signing his treaty with the Indians. These textiles were very popular and found their way into many sets of curtains and bed furnishings. Family history relates that Sarah Anderson made this quilt top from parlor curtains purchased from "a sale of Major Carneal's father [after she came to Kentucky]...." (Note from accession information of the Kentucky Historical Society.) The back, it further states, "...was made from flax grown on Grandma

Sarah Runyan Anderson's father's place in new Yersey [sic], and spun and woven by Grandma Anderson (Sarah Runyan)." One would guess she brought with her to Kentucky finished linen sheets made by her in New Jersey. Such salvaging and reuse was common; good textiles were expensive if bought or took much energy and time to make. Special bought material might be used for an important quilt, or colorful sections used to liven up a quilt composed mostly of lesser cloths;–a little bit could go a long way visually.

Kirtley had been born near Smiths Grove and he had three brothers fighting for the Confederacy. The letter relates that one of the brothers, Paschal, was shot in the leg at Shiloh. He died of complications from the wound.

A second brother was killed in a battle near Munfordville. "I think he was with Morgan's Brigade," the letter says. "His body was buried in the trench with the other casualties."

The third brother was wounded at Vicksburg. "He was nursed back to health by one of the First families of the South," the letter says. "On the eve of his return home, he was struck by lightning and killed. He lies buried in Vicksburg Cemetery."

John Kirtley, the only one of the brothers who didn't volunteer for the Confederate army, eventually was drafted by the Union army. He was allowed to send a substitute, and he hired one of his father's former slaves to serve in his place.

Kirtley survived the war, and so did the slave who went off to fight in his stead. Kirtley's father is said to have gone somewhat mad, however. Toward the end of the war he gave himself the title of "general" and gathered about him some men who had soured on both the Union and the Confederacy. Together they roamed the countryside, sniping at soldiers of any and all persuasions.

It was precisely to avoid such conflict and unrest that many families stayed out of Kentucky during their migration west. Margaret Silbersack Geiger would marry and live out her life on a farm in northern Kentucky, but she was born in 1861 in Delhi, Ohio, just below Cincinnati on the Ohio River. Like many immigrants who had left the Rhine valley of Germany for the Ohio valley of America, Margaret's parents settled north of the river to wait out the war, then bought farms in Kentucky. (Plate 35.)

Throughout the 1800s and into the early part of the twentieth century, the character of the Kentucky countryside remained predominantly rural, and the interests of families like the Geigers were aligned closely with the demands and the needs of the land. Each thing had its time, planting and harvesting and building, and often neighbors shared such labors. In western Kentucky, the Stewart and Burgess families had been drawn together by marriages in the nineteenth century. The families lived on farms that covered about 1,000 acres near the Cumberland River. They raised hogs, sheep, cattle, horses–prize horses–and mules, among other things.

fig. 8. Margaret Silbersack, who constructed the Four Patch quilt, is shown in a photograph taken about the time of her 1882 marriage to John Geiger. Plate 35.

❋ *Plate 36. Detail of plate 35.*

✻ Plate 37. Lily variation. Pieced and appliqué quilt. Made by a member of either the Stewart or Burgess families. Trigg County, Kentucky. Circa 1865. Cotton. 88" x 72". Collection of Lofton Alexander.

This is a clever arrangement of the popular Lily pattern, stylized flowers of piecework on appliqué stems, arranged in groups of three. Here the design has been arranged so that each cluster forms at its center a white six-pointed star. The ability to make such original variations was a great strength of American quiltmakers. This quilt was clearly executed by a superior seamstress. The design is original, confident, and beautifully realized, potentially difficult edges have been brilliantly resolved, the whole is harmonious and forceful. Often quiltmakers working closely together, as evidently they did in the Stewart and Burgess families, spur outstanding creators to greater achievement, a phenomenon which occurs in all types of creative endeavor.

Nearly everyone in the two families lived on three adjoining farms. When a son or daughter married, a room would be added to the main farmhouse for the use of the new couple. The men helped one another in the fields; the women canned and cooked together, and they got together for quilting.

The women of the Stewart and Burgess families were, in fact, members of a floating quilting bee that seemed ever to be in session at one or another of the families' farms. Quilts were made for newlyweds and grandchildren, and they were made as gifts for non-family members as well. They were made for the most utilitarian of reasons, and they were made for special occasions. Above all else, they were made as a joint effort of the Stewart and Burgess women. The precise authorship of each quilt remains unclear, however, because different women made up the groups that worked on each quilt. (Plates 37 and 38.)

❋ *Plate 38. Rose appliqué quilt. Made by a member of either the Stewart or Burgess family. Trigg County, Kentucky. Circa 1865. Cotton. 96" x 81". Collection of Lofton Alexander.*

A second superb quilt from the Stewart-Burgess families, this one is also a masterful floral composition but completely different in effect from the angular, geometric field of the Lily quilt, Plate 37. The surface is really quite jammed with images, but skillful organization has made it lively and visually satisfying when it might have been merely busy. It is interesting that both naturalistic and abstracted images of similar subjects were made in the same era, often by the same quiltmaker. They seemed to have had no difficulty moving from one manner of seeing and executing images to another, helped perhaps by the organizing influence of the square, the basis of a large percentage of quilts. The red-and-green-on-white combination was a favorite for good appliqué quilts in all parts of the country during the period.

In *Agrarian Kentucky,* Clark writes that the "whole tenor of Kentucky rural existence was governed by the changing seasons." One farm wife, Mary Louisa Givens Midkiff, who was known as Lula, kept a daily log that reflects the all-pervasive importance of the weather on rural life. Here are typical entries:

"April 6: Ground frozen some this morning. Snowed again. Raining tonight. Lena here this morning. Bernice this afternoon. Too bad for farmers to do anything.

May 30: We had services at the school house this morning. Brother Chism preached a good sermon. Bernice and Lillian Gilmore here this morning. We had an electrical storm, good rain and some hail this eve. Wrote to the kids. Got 578 eggs this month.

June 8: Washed this morning, got dinner and churned. Grant finished breaking the garden and plowed the other part out. We planted more corn and beans and the late potatoes. Bernice here this eve. Joe Howe brought us some sweet potato slips this morn." (Plate 39.)

In north-central Kentucky, another farm wife, Sophronia Ann Bruce, tended a large garden and raised turkeys. One of her daughters, Fannie, lived in the Ohio

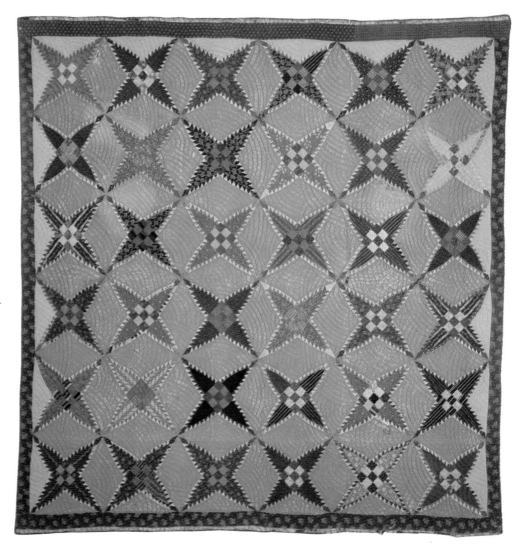

❀ *Plate 39. Star variant. Pieced quilt. Made by Mary Louise Givens Midkiff. Hancock County, Kentucky. Circa 1895. Cotton. 80" x 75". Collection of Mr. and Mrs. James Stephen Allison.*

A pleasing version of the four-pointed star with a miniature Nine patch block at each center and a pieced sawtooth edging on each star, the latter an ambitious embellishment that adds considerably to the visual impact of the image. The highly visible quilting, blocks of curved parallel lines that intersect to form wavelike patterns across the quilt, add depth and movement to the surface. The cottons would have been used for dresses and shirts. This quilt was meant to be a serviceable, washable, everyday bedcover. The efficient production of such covers encouraged great design innovation.

❋ *Plate 40. Honeycomb or Mosaic. Pieced and appliqué quilt with stuffed work and padding. Made by Sophronia Ann Bruce. Henry County, Kentucky. Circa 1880. Cotton, wool, and silk. 107" x 92". Collection of Mrs. Ronda G. Taylor.*

The quilt has some unusual elements: The swag border is of a type normally used with an appliqué quilt but has here been added to a pieced quilt; the mixture of materials is not often seen; and it is unusual to use padded work in such generous border elements. In addition the maker used the Honeycomb or Mosaic pieces, usually combined into an over-all rosette pattern, to create a ten-pointed star, most unusual if not unique.

This is a pieced quilt clearly meant to be as important as a "best" appliqué quilt. A great deal of time went into making the elaborate stuffed work, floral pots and sprays, and grape clusters. Sophronia Bruce had a very particular vision and the courage to work in opposition to accepted formats.

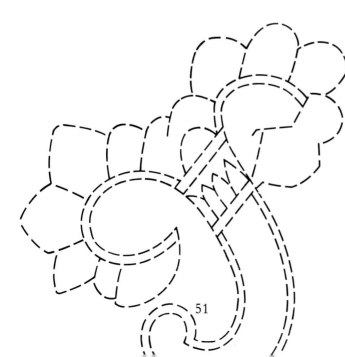

River bottom and survived two of the biggest floods in the river's history–in February 1883 and February 1884. Sophronia's letters to Fannie reflect a constant worry about her daughter's safety along the river, but they also are filled with accounts of other concerns of rural women.

"Friday eve, Hallie [another daughter] and myself went down to Thomas's place to get some peaches. Gathering and beating off the trees made us so sore that we can hardly get about. Yesterday we made a gallon of preserves and canned six quarts."

On a February morning in 1885, when the temperature outside stood at 10 degrees below zero, Sophronia wrote Fannie:

"Well, last eve I took the neuralgia in my breast and had to stop writing and go to doctoring. I just take a flannel cloth and grease it with lard and put turpentine on it and heat an iron and hold it on for half an hour; and that relieves it. Try it if ever you have it. Oh, it is so cold this morn, we can hardly keep warm by the fire." (Plate 40.)

51

The cold, the hardships, and the isolation from prompt medical attention made death a commonplace part of rural life. Richard H. Collins's 1882 *History of Kentucky* has entry after entry devoted to accounts of deaths by cholera and other diseases.

An apparent preoccupation with death led to the creation of the famous Graveyard Quilt by Elizabeth Roseberry Mitchell in 1839. Mrs. Mitchell and her husband were natives of Pennsylvania and in 1831 they moved with their family to southeast Ohio, near the Ohio River. Two of their sons died there and in 1834 the Mitchells moved to northeast Kentucky.

Mrs. Mitchell visited the old home in Ohio four years later and she is said to have grieved deeply over the two sons buried there. When she returned to Kentucky, she made the quilt, with its cemetery, its coffins, and its somber browns. The graveyard at its center encompasses coffins bearing the names of dead members of the family, and the coffins lined up at the entrance bear the names of family members still living at that time. The apparent intention was for these latter coffins to be moved into the graveyard as the family members died. (Plate 42.)

❋ *Plate 41. Framed center in Star motif. Pieced quilt with embroidery. Kentucky. Circa 1890. Velvet. 89" x 89". Collection of Nancy Starr.*

This format, a central square holding the main image surrounded by borders often repeating the same image and fancy corners, is not usually seen in quilts this late. It is a throwback to a quilt style of a century earlier and employs star images which are among the most venerable in the pieced quilter's visual repertoire. The unusual overall velvet surface catches the light nicely.

✻ Plate 42. The Graveyard Quilt. Star of Lemoyne with graveyard in the center and caskets on three sides. Pieced and appliqué quilt with embroidery. Made by Elizabeth Roseberry Mitchell. Lewis County, Kentucky. Circa 1839. Cotton. 85" x 81". Collection of the Kentucky Historical Society, Frankfort, Kentucky. Accession number 59.13.

This is a famous folk object–as well it should be. There are few to equal it as examples of obsessive art. According to family history, Elizabeth Mitchell made this after visiting the graves of two sons who had died some years before in Ohio. Not content with creating burial space just for them on her quilt, however,

she provided the little burial plot in the center with spaces carefully marked out in quilting for thirteen coffins. And she thoughtfully fashioned twenty-one other coffins, conveniently labeled for family members, around the edges of the quilt. It appears that two of them were moved in to join her boys after the quilt was made. The significance of the quilt could be endlessly debated; certainly it expresses a view of life profoundly affected by the loss of loved ones, and by the high mortality rate of the times. While many lived to advanced ages, many, many more died at a younger age than is our experience. The quilt is bound by picket fences. The outer one encloses a spirit world. Just

inside is a barrier of labeled and quilted waiting coffins; the living wish to go no farther. The inner fence rings the abode of the dead, a fenced walk and gate, its entrance. It looks like the board for some macabre game.

In a sense this is a memorial quilt, perhaps made to expunge the grief of Elizabeth's loss and assuage her fear of those to come. While it is a unique quilt, other death-related art in textiles and other media was made during the period, painted and embroidered mourning and memorial pictures, elaborate tombstones, etc. One curious thing is that it shows a good bit of wear, and one wonders who found it warming to sleep under it.

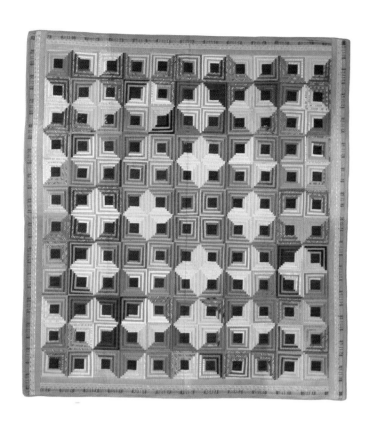

❋ Plate 43. Log Cabin block
arranged in a pattern called Sunshine and Shadow. Pieced quilt.
Made by Martha Tribble Hieatt.
Henry County, Kentucky. Circa
1875. Silk. 81" x 76". Collection
of Patricia Ricketts O'Flynn.

The Log Cabin block is uniquely
constructed. It usually has a foundation and strips of material sewn each
to the next in a manner reminiscent
of log cabin construction. It always
has a square center–red the first
color preference, yellow the second–
and is divided diagonally–one-half
of dark materials, one-half of light.
The blocks can then be arranged in
a number of different configurations
which give completely different
overall effects. This one is called
"Sunshine and Shadow" for obvious
reasons. "Barn Raising" and
"Straight Furrow" are two others.
Whatever the arrangement, it is
always visually effective and has
been the basis for some of our greatest pieced quilts.

fig. 9. The silk Log Cabin quilt
was constructed by Martha Tribble
Hieatt, photographed here in 1880.
Plate 43.

54

Death also was an all-too-frequent visitor in the life of Martha Tribble. She married a widower, William Hieatt, in 1846, and twelve years later, her husband and three daughters died, the girls of scarlet fever. Only one of six children survived Martha Tribble Hieatt, and when she died in 1901, at the age of eighty, the local newspaper wrote:

"Comment on her life is superfluous. It was a full, glorious one, and she was ripe for the harvest of the gathering angel. Beyond the chilling gulf of death, she has joined her family in the home of her God, whom here she served nobly." (Plate 43.)

❧ *Plate 44. Detail of plate 43.*

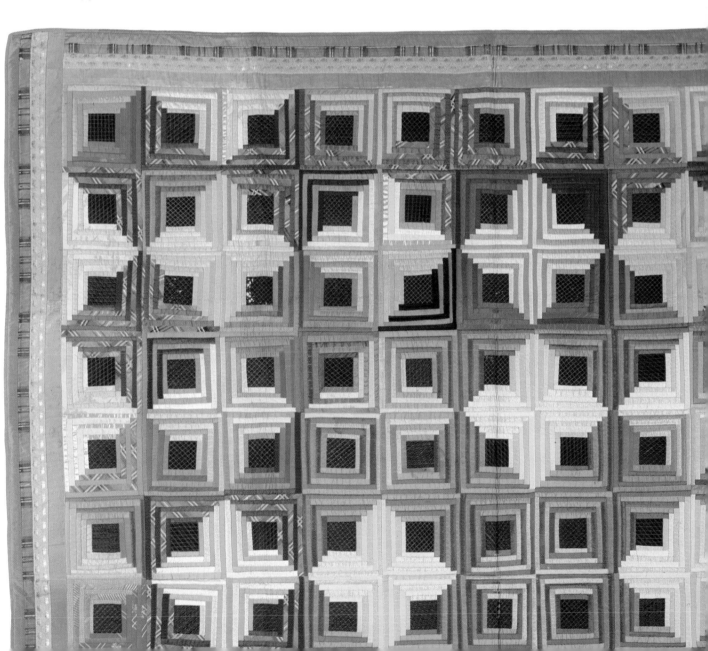

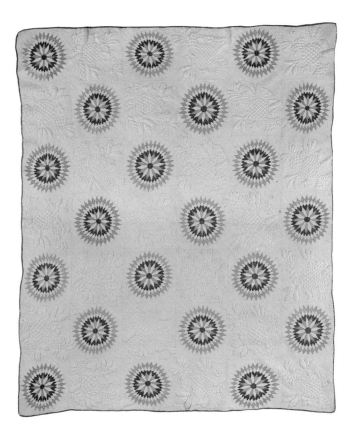

Plate 46. Sunburst. Pieced quilt with stuffed work. Made by Elizabeth Taylor Brawner Perkins. Somerset, Kentucky. Circa 1865. Cotton. 86" x 74". Collection of Mary E. Kaurish.

The many-rayed star appears very early in American quilts and is seen in many forms. It was a favorite design in New England in the form of the Mariner's Compass. Such intricate star patterns are quite exacting to make so are often reserved for best quilts. This quilt is clearly one of those–time has been lavished on stuffed-work pineapples, the sign of hospitality, and its large areas of white, easily soiled, mean it was not meant for everyday use. Sometimes such quilts were reserved for guests. Circular motifs widely spaced on a white ground were commonly used when an elegant effect was desired.

Women who married at an early age all too often were widowed at an early age. At Somerset, in south–central Kentucky, Elizabeth Taylor made a Sunburst quilt for her dowry and then married, about 1838, at the age of fifteen. Her husband was a Captain Brawner, who had fought a few years earlier in the Texas war of independence.

Many of Kentucky's pioneer families had moved on to Texas to take advantage of the Mexican government's offer of low-priced land. There also were free land bounties to men who brought in parties of settlers. Clark wrote: "As early as 1825 there was a "Texas Emigration Society" in Lexington through whose influence many settlers were sent to the Southwest. So enthusiastic were many Kentuckians over Texas that women volunteers were collected and sent to the Southwest to become wives of adventurous single males who had moved there from Kentucky."

By 1844, according to Clark, a large percentage of the 50,000 American settlers in Texas were Kentuckians.

Captain Brawner survived the war in Texas, but he died shortly after his marriage, and for many years Elizabeth was known as "the widow Brawner." She later remarried–and outlived–Dr. John Milton Perkins. Their home, which is on the National Register of Historic Places, is next door to the public library in Somerset. (Plate 46.)

fig. 10. Eliza Ann and George Mattingly are shown, circa 1900, in the yard of their farm home. She created the Wheel of Fortune quilt. Plate 47.

Subsistence farms, though most prevalent in the mountains, were common across the breadth of Kentucky. Eliza and George Mattingly had a farm near Grayson Springs, in west–central Kentucky. Because of its twenty-four mineral wells, Grayson Springs had become something of a resort town. The first hotel was built there in 1836, and before the Civil War the community was a summering place for a number of well-to-do families from the South.

Eliza Ann Mattingly supplemented the meager farm income by doing washing and ironing for families who stayed at the resort; her family sold strawberries to the hotel for 20 cents a gallon. (Plate 47.)

Hard times on subsistence farms meant that clothes, furnishings, utensils, and other household items got used far beyond their normal life span. In *What My Heart Wants to Tell*, Verna Mae Slone wrote about growing up in the mountains of eastern Kentucky and says:
"When quilts had outgrown their usefulness for the beds, they made saddle blankets, covers for a chicken coop, a dog bed, or they were hung over the opening of the outhouse or barn in place of a door shutter, or placed on the floor as a pallet for the baby."

Mrs. Slone also wrote about the skills that her mother knew–skills that virtually all rural Kentucky women learned from their mothers and then tried to pass on to their daughters.
"As for "book learnin," my mother knew only one letter, the letter "O." But she was educated in the things she needed to know: how to raise a family; how to card wool and spin it to yarn; how to dye the yarn with bark and roots gathered from the hillside, which of these to use to get the color she wanted; and how to knit this yarn into stockings and caps for her husband and children. With some help, she sheared wool from her own sheep.

She knew when to plant her garden, which plants grow better in one soil than another, when to fertilize–using manure from the barn and chicken house and rotten cinders and ashes from the fireplace–and how much was needed.

❀ *Plate 47. Rising Sun. (Family name for this design: Wheel of Fortune.) Pieced and appliqué quilt. Made by Eliza Ann Mattingly. Grayson Springs, Kentucky. Circa 1860. Cotton. 100" x 80". Collection of Mabel Frank.*

This is an ambitious pattern because of the many curved lines; it requires a practiced hand to sew them without puckers. The little appliquéd circle at the center of each square resolves the design and hides the ends of the spokes, which would be almost impossible to bring together in a neat and visually satisfactory manner. Each square is edged with a pieced sawtooth border, which nicely sets off the central image. Such basically blue-on-white quilts are always effective visually; the combination is a serene one, and when the scale and drawing of the design is as well accomplished as it is here, the effect is both vital and elegant.

She loved to make her rows of beans and peas as straight as an arrow, dragging up large "ridges" or beds for her sweet potatoes, beets and parsnips. She had artistic interest in how pretty she could make them look. She knew how to grow all the different vegetables, when to plant, to hoe and gather them. She knew how to dry the green beans, to make shuck beans and how to dry the "punkin" and cushaw (crookneck squash) for winter use. She sliced them into rings, about an inch wide, and hung them from a pole over the fireplace. She would have large barrels of shelled beans for soup beans. She knew how to make sauerkraut and pickled corn and beans.

She had a very large garden–row after row of vegetables–but the very best, with the richest soil, she used for her flowers: fall roses (zinnias), marigolds, bachelor's buttons, and touch-me-nots, and many others, too many to name."

59

Religion was the traditional solace of rural women in hard times and good. As early as 1800, religious revivals in Kentucky had attracted sizeable crowds. The Cane Ridge campground meeting, in August 1801, is said to have drawn 20,000 people to central Kentucky. Collins' history reports that "3,000 people, mostly men, [were] computed to have fallen and experienced remarkable bodily exercises" at the revival.

Of all the denominations, the Baptists reached farthest and deepest into rural Kentucky society, and when hard economic times befell the Kentucky Baptist Orphans Home, church members decided upon a quilt project to bail the institution out. A quilt of eighty-one nine-inch squares was decided upon, with each square to be sold to individuals, churches and organizations for a minimum of $18.

The project raised $5,000, and in 1882 the Kentucky Baptist Orphans Home quilt was assembled from the squares, each of which had been embroidered by or in memory of Baptist churches, Sunday school classes, associations, and members from all over Kentucky. (Plate 49.)

Plate 49. Block crazy. Pieced and appliqué church revenue quilt with embroidery. Louisville, Kentucky. Made by various Baptist groups. Dated 1882. Satin, velvet, and silk. 96" x 96". Collection of the Kentucky Baptist Homes for Children.

A crazy-type quilt built in block rather than the more usual random form. It was constructed this way because it was a friendship-style quilt, with many different groups working on blocks, and an overall format had to be chosen in advance so it would come together correctly at the end. Squares are the easiest way to insure this. Each group making a block contributed $18, a handsome sum then. The visual confusion of the Crazy quilt style is emphasized here because the design elements are framed up like a series of completely different little pictures. As in many Crazy quilts, one ends up sorting through the images to find the most pleasing ones. The floral sprays, bouquets, and wreaths seem particularly well realized.

Churches also raised money with quilts. Groups within the churches working communally would create quilts to be raffled at picnics and ice cream socials. The Altar Society of St. Charles Catholic Church in Louisville made a number of such quilts. But church members made a special presentation quilt for St. Charles Founding Priest, Rev. C. P. Raffo, and presented it to him April 3, 1899. (Plate 51.)

❉ *Plate 50. Detail of plate 51.*

❉ *Plate 51. Friendship autograph quilt. Made by members of St. Charles Church, Louisville, Kentucky. Dated 1899. Cotton. 108" x 72". Collection of Elaine Sloan Hart.*

Members of Rev. C. P. Raffo's congregation at St. Charles Church in Louisville made this quilt for him and presented it on Easter Monday, 1899. Friendship quilts, produced as communal projects and carrying the names of the participants, were made for different purposes in a variety of styles. Some honored a friend leaving a community, or a betrothal, or, according to tradition, in the form of a "freedom" quilt, the end of a boy's apprenticeship. Autograph quilts were another form, used by churches to raise money; a person payed so much for the privilege of having his signature embroidered on (sometimes with the amount of his contribution). The quilt could then be auctioned or raffled, which raised further revenue. Churches in America have long been centers for quilting activities in the forms both of revenue-raising projects (making quilts for sale and quilting on commission) and social occasions (many groups meet simply for the pleasures of the company and the work).

fig. 11. Sallie Crain Garr, photographed here in 1912, was the maker of the Crazy quilt embroidered with the year of her marriage, 1883, to Dr. Charles Russell Garr. Plate 53.

A devotion to religion and family was hardly confined to rural women, as is readily apparent from the daily journal kept by Sallie Crain Garr. The daughter of a well-to-do Hillsboro, Kentucky, merchant, she was married to Dr. Charles Russell Garr, a physician who one day would own the first automobile in Fleming County.

Sallie Garr's journal covers a wide span of her years, from before her sons were born to after they were married and after her husband had died. On different New Year's days, she wrote:

"Jan. 1, 1888: This is my 26th birthday. My life has been one sweet happy dream.

Jan. 1, 1889: This is my 27th birthday. I am so thankful for my happy home and my sweet boys. So many changes since my last birthday–the greatest and saddest–the loss of our dear mother.

Jan. 1, 1902: Can it be that I have reached the age of 40? The Lord has smiled on me all my life." (Plate 53.)

❋ *Plate 53. Crazy. Pieced and appliqué quilt with added embroidery. Made by Sarah Crain Garr. Hillsboro, Kentucky. Dated 1883. Silk, velvet, paper. 77" x 75". Collection of Elizabeth Garr Lawrence.*

Sarah Crain made this quilt the year of her marriage to Dr. Charles Garr, and it appears to be both a family memento and a celebration of the new family she was forming. There is her last name and Garr family initials, some standard Crazy quilt imagery (the umbrella, fan, horseshoe, shamrock, bonneted young girl, and female boot) and then images probably of particular interest to her and her families, a mitten, gingerbread figures, a silk portrait of Sir Walter Scott. There was great interest in the Orient, especially Japan, during the period, and that is the source of some of the imagery. The maker included some printed Japanese paper pieces in the quilt.

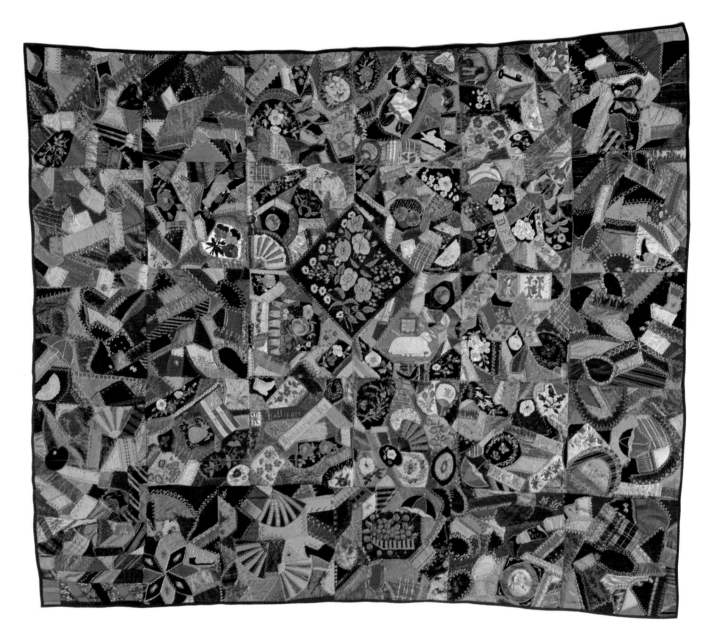

❋ Plate 54. Crazy. Pieced quilt with embroidery and three-dimensional work. Made by Lizzie Hollinger. Henderson, Kentucky. Dated 1885. Silk and velvet. 86″ x 103″. Collection of Shelly Zegart.

Made at a time when fussy Victorian design sensibilities were at their height, this quilt is a showcase of the type. It is of silk and velvet dress materials in a random pattern (the word "crazy" means crazed, as in pottery or glass, rather than insane), with the most elaborate profusion of stitches and decoration possible. It has many of the sentimental motifs popular during the period and often seen on such quilts–a baby's crib, fans, parasols, flowers (especially pansies and violets and roses), butterflies, artists palettes–all rendered in embroidery or three-dimensional padded work. In the latter techniques there are flowers, a pear, peaches singly and in a basket, a whole box of strawberries. In such quilts one can always find the images that haunted the Victorian subconscious–the spider in his web, innocent children at play, the key, the Lamb of God, provocative women's boots. And, of course, the family, the maker's name, town and date, and children or siblings, Mary, William, Lizzie, Dan, Batie.

66

❋ *Plate 55. Detail of plate 54.*

As the nineteenth century progressed, more and more Kentucky women lived in towns and cities. By 1860, Louisville was the main urban center, and the Civil War helped solidify its dominance. Clark wrote:

"Fortunately for Louisville, Mother Nature had placed her in the mouth of the funnel of trade down the Ohio Valley to the South. Louisville was located strategically to control the livestock and supply trade southward, and she showed the advantages of this ideal location by growing from a village of 4,000, in 1820, to a city of 100,000, in 1870, and 307,745, in 1930."

❋ *Plate 56. Detail of plate 54.*

Retail merchants and tradesmen were naturally attracted to such population centers. Andrew August Schmidt and Marie Theresia Hagedorn, who came to the United States from Germany, met and married in New York City, then came down the river to open a grocery store in Louisville. In 1872 they had a daughter, Anna Marie.

Edmund Steinbock, an apprentice tailor, came to the United States from Germany at the age of sixteen, and he settled in Louisville because a great aunt lived there–not far from Anna Marie Schmidt, as it turned out. Steinbock and Anna Marie were married in 1890, and her Crazy Quilt–dated that same year–apparently was made as a memento of her own family.

After her marriage, Anna Marie worked in Steinbock's tailor shop, sewing linings and padding into men's suits, and they lived in the same building. There was a kitchen and dining room in back of the shop; the parlor and bedrooms were upstairs. (Plate 58.)

fig. 12. Anna Marie Schmidt, creator of the Crazy quilt, was dressed for her first communion in this photograph, circa 1885. Plate 58.

❉ *Plate 57. Detail of plate 58.*

❋ Plate 58. Crazy. Pieced quilt with embroidery and three-dimensional cloth flowers. Made by Anna Marie Steinbock. Louisville, Kentucky. Dated 1890. Silk and velvet. 89" x 84". Collection of Elizabeth Steinbock Mills.

Anna Marie Schmidt made this quilt the year of her marriage to Edmund Steinbock near the end of the long Victorian era. The quilt has been given a little more organization than is usual for the type through the use of a border to confine the busy surface and a middle section around which the quilt

is built. At the center, arranged on pennants flying from a square enclosing a bouquet of three-dimensional flowers, is the family, arranged, no doubt, in order of age: Father, Mother, Willie, Josephine, Henry, Augusta, Annie, and George.

The family was at the center of proper Victorian life–perhaps even more so for Europeans than Americans and especially for first and second-generation immigrants adjusting to the American pace and ways. It gave a sense of stability and safety in a world that was moving from the measured beat of an agrar-

ian society to the faster tempo of an industrialized one. Only female children seem to have survived in the family–the boys are in heaven, their names held by angels. One can see on the quilt many of the stock Victorian images–birds, violets, pansies and roses, little girls, fans, a horse-shoe, spiderwebs, butterflies—all embellished with the usual profusion of stitches. Such crazy quilts are a distinct type, made during a relatively short period as decorative, not functional, textiles, whose primary purpose was to serve as a family album and demonstrate the maker's knowledge of Victorian sensibilities.

In this case it appears to have been made to go with Anna ("Annie") as a memento of her family. Family history indicates it was made by her, but it is possible that it was made for her by both of the other women in the family or that it was a family project.

❀ *Plate 59. Detail of plate 60.*

Louisville also was home to many families whose affluence stemmed from their positions in commerce or industry. Neighborhoods full of grand homes sprang up in the late nineteenth century.

George Garvin Brown, founder of the Brown-Forman Distillers Corporation, and Amelia Owsley Brown lived in a mansion across from Central Park. A butler named Herbert lived in the carriage house on the back of the property. Among his other duties, Herbert did the needlework for the household, and he is thought to have created the Brown quilt. (Plate 60.)

70

✻ Plate 60. Rose of Sharon. Appliqué quilt with padded work. According to Brown family tradition, made by a butler, Herbert. Louisville, Kentucky. Circa 1865. Cotton. 93" x 93". Collection of Amelia Payne Sweets Runyon.

Family tradition gives the making of this quilt to a man, a butler named Herbert, and that would make it rare indeed. Very few American quilts have been documented as male handiwork, though some number were no doubt made by men. In general, in this country, sewing was a female pursuit, and the rare cases of male quilters we have come across indicates they were normally invalids or older men who could not do robust work but wished to keep active. A few histories of male-made quilts describe their making as "therapy" for men recovering from the shock of war.

This is an extremely lively version of the beloved Rose of Sharon design, one made in many variations. The extremely curved stems, so bowed that the heads turn back to the ground, and the crowded surface create a feeling of movement. The flower groups look like dancers. Usually such quilts are more serene. The swag border, a folk adaption of a refined Federal border, was meant to add an elegant touch. The flower heads and buds are rendered in padded work, a technique for creating three-dimensional effects in which the part to be filled out is appliquéd to the quilt top and the filler put in just before the last stitches are done.

❀ *Plate 61. Daisy. Pieced and reverse appliqué quilt. Made by a member of the Brennan family. Louisville, Kentucky. Circa 1900. Cotton. 82" x 77". Collection of The Filson Club, Louisville, Kentucky.*

This elegant quilt uses a rare technique–reverse appliqué–for the heads of the flowers. A section of the top was backed with the blue material, then the long ovals that form the flower's head were cut away from the top to show the blue underneath and the opening finished with a buttonhole stitch. The quilting is remarkable both in quality and design; the maker used a variety of motifs–flowers, cable, grid, and pinwheel on the interior, large pineapples on the outer edges. Pineapples had been a symbol of hospitality since Colonial days, and their inclusion on a quilt sometimes marked it as one used for the guest bed. Such white quilts, so easy to soil, were reserved for special beds or special occasions.

The Brennan House, a landmark in downtown Louisville, was bought by Thomas Brennan in 1884. Brennan had settled in Louisville shortly after arriving in the United States from Ireland in the 1850s. He is thought to have been something of a mechanical genius, for he held a number of patents, including those for the cider press and the sorghum mill.

In 1869 Brennan was married to Anna Virginia Bruce, a well-read woman whose father was an Episcopal priest. Born on the Isle of Jersey, she taught school in Louisville after the Civil War.

❋ Plate 62. White quilt with stuffed work and cording. Made by Willie Sharpe Fink with the assistance of her sister-in-law and mother-in-law. Mercer County, Kentucky. Circa 1875. Cotton. 82" x 70". Collection of The Kentucky Museum, Bowling Green, Kentucky. Record number 1806.

Such elaborate white quilts were especially popular in America, though never common, in the second half of the nineteenth century. Design was always elaborate, but it never seems too much in these quilts; this is a case where more can be better. Often there is an involved floral centerpiece, a bouquet or basket of flowers and fruit. This quilt is actually quite restrained as the type goes, with a single open flower at the center surrounded by grapevines, clusters, and leaves, with other grape designs filling the ground, sunflowers in each quarter, and hearts along the sides. The raised effects were achieved with stuffed work and cording. In stuffed work the area to be filled is outlined in stitches that go through both top and back. Stuffing is then introduced into the area a little at a time through separated rows of threads in the back or through a small slit in the back, later closed. The vines were done in cording, in which a cord is introduced to the surface of the quilt through a channel prepared for it or is laid on and covered, as in padded work. The background of the quilt, as was considered desirable, is practically quilted away. Family history states it took twelve dozen spools of thread of accomplish this. The grape motifs–vines, leaves, and tendrils–have been rendered with great fidelity; the whole effect is sinuous and lively.

The Brennan quilt apparently was made for the Brennans' son Bruce, born in 1885. Its blue daisy pattern, in reverse appliqué, reflects refinement, civility, and sophistication, a sign that Louisville had come a long way since the early settlers had struck out for new homes over the dusty "Kaintuck Hog Road." (Plate 61.)

Ms. Irvin says that she wrote her book about women in Kentucky because "women were there, their lives are worth looking at, and often they contributed more than they are given credit for." By the end of the century they had begun to battle their invisibility, speaking out for suffrage, higher education, property rights. But for most their testament remains their diaries and letters, their memories held as verbal histories by their families, and, often most eloquently, the things they made. Glimpses of their lives through these things are snapshots of Kentucky history.

73

Bibliography

Channing, Steven A. *Kentucky.* New York: W. W. Norton & Company, Inc., 1977.

Clark, Thomas D. *A History of Kentucky.* Lexington, Kentucky: The John Bradford Press, 1954.

Clark, Thomas D. *Agrarian Kentucky.* Lexington, Kentucky: The University Press of Kentucky, 1977.

Clarke, Mary Washington. *Kentucky Quilts and Their Makers.* Lexington, Kentucky: The University Press of Kentucky, 1976.

Collins, Lewis, and Richard H. Collins. *History of Kentucky.* Covington, Kentucky: Collins & Co., 1882.

Irvin, Helen Deiss. *Women in Kentucky.* Lexington, Kentucky: The University Press of Kentucky, 1979.

Slone, Verna Mae. *What My Heart Wants to Tell.* Washington, D.C.: New Republic Books, 1979.

Lenders

❊ At the date of publication, these quilts are scheduled to tour with the Smithsonian Institution Traveling Exhibition Service.

Quotation marks are used for the family names of quilts when differing from the cataloged name.

Special Thanks

A special thank you to the following people who have assisted The Kentucky Quilt Project 1800-1900, Inc., and whose help contributed greatly to the success of the Project:

The Staff and Board of Directors of the Museum of History and Science, Louisville, Kentucky, and the Smithsonian Institution Traveling Exhibition Service, Washington, D.C.

Organizations
Kentucky Heritage Quilt Society, Inc.
Louisville Nimble Thimbles, Inc. (N. Q. A. Affiliate)
Embroiderers Guild of America, Louisville Chapter

Quilt Day Organizers and Locations
Ashland, Kentucky–Celeste Winters, Paramount Arts Center
Bowling Green, Kentucky–Anne Johnston, The Kentucky Museum
Covington, Kentucky–Chris Kellogg, Northern Kentucky Arts Council
Hopkinsville, Kentucky–Betty Smith, Hopkinsville-Christian County Library
Lexington, Kentucky–Nancy Wolsk, Morlan Gallery, Transylvania University
Louisville, Kentucky–Janice Rossano, Dorothy West, Art Center Association
Owensboro, Kentucky–Margie Herreld, Owensboro Area Museum
Paducah, Kentucky–Michael Watts, Paducah Art Guild
Somerset, Kentucky–Bennie Newton, Mary Vance Day, Pulaski County Public Library, and United American Bank
Whitesburg, Kentucky–Josephine Richardson, Graham Memorial Presbyterian Church

Museums
The Kentucky Historical Society, Frankfort, Kentucky
The Kentucky Museum, Western Kentucky University, Bowling Green, Kentucky
A special thank you to Dorothy Stites, The Indianapolis Museum of Art, and Lois Vann, Textile Division, The Smithsonian Institution, for their instruction in quilt preparation.

Quilts Prepared for Exhibit by:

Ellen E. Allen	Mary Neuschwander
Su Bachert	Karen C. Ogden
Ann M. Bischoff	Thames Palmer-Ball
Deanna K. Bond	Iris B. Peers
Marty Bowman	Marsha Peuce
Sue Bredensteiner	Jean Peniston
Mary Pat Carroll	Joy Peterson
Ann S. Coates	Nancy Ragland
Mary Anderson Courtenay	Sue Robare
Teresa Dobson	Lysa Scarborough
Sally Forcade	Judy Scott
Denise Furnish	Pat Scovile
Jane Gentry	Pat Sturtzel
Helen Hamblin	Helen Thompson
Barbara Harp	Alexis Tibbs
Helen S. Hess	Muriel Trowbridge
Jane A. Hewitt	Evelyn Vittitow
Mary Jewett	Lucy Wheeler
Starr Kaiser	Charlotte Willis
Mary Julia Kuhn	Mary Lee Younger

A Very Special Thanks to:
Anne Gossett, Smithsonian Institution Traveling Exhibition Service, Washington, D.C.
Riley Handy, The Kentucky Museum, Bowling Green, Kentucky
Elaine "Cissy" Musselman, Louisville, Kentucky
Elizabeth Perkins, The Kentucky Historical Society, Frankfort, Kentucky
Nikko Pitanis, Lexington, Kentucky
Matilda Wells Andrews, Louisville, Kentucky
Alan E. Sears , Louisville, Kentucky

Production Team

Directors
Eleanor Bingham Miller
Eunice Ray
Shelly Zegart

Consultant
Katy Christopherson

Project Coordinator
Dorothy West

Exhibition Curator
Nancy Comstock

Staff
Marcia Martin
Janice Rossano
Dru Cawood

Quilt Days Photographers
Roea Wallace
David Cronen

Fig 14. Seated from left to right:
Eunice Ray, Shelly Zegart,
Standing from left to right:
Eleanor Miller, Katy Christopherson,
Dorothy West

The Authors

Jonathan Holstein was born in Syracuse, New York in 1936. He saw around him as he grew up the products of skilled American craftsmen, furniture, woven and sewn textiles, pottery and glass, as well as the works and historical remains of the Iroquois. This began a lifelong interest in Americana. He had begun to collect before he went to Harvard University, from which he graduated, an English major, in 1958. Work at McGraw Hill Publishing Company in New York followed, and a stint as a photographer of fine art. In 1969 he and his future wife, Gail van der Hoof, became interested in the aesthetics of American quilts; many a century or more old seemed to them strikingly modern visually. Researching here and abroad and collecting intensively, they formed a large collection from which was drawn many museum exhibitions which appeared in both the U.S. and other countries, the first in 1971 at the Whitney Museum of American Art in New York. These exhibitions began the interest in American quilts as a design form and helped spark a general rebirth of interest in the subject. In 1972 his book, *The Pieced Quilt: An American Design Tradition,* a basic study of quilts, was published, and many exhibition catalogs, articles and lectures followed. He has pursued his interest in the American Indian professionally and has been for some years a private dealer in Native American art.

John Finley is a twenty-year veteran of newspaper journalism, spending the last fourteen years writing for *The Courier-Journal* in Louisville. He has held a variety of writing and editing assignments in the newspaper business and while at *The Courier-Journal* was awarded the 1969 Emery A. Brownell Press Award of the National Legal Aid and Defender Association, the 1974 Louisville Bar Association Gavel Award for legal reporting, the 1974 award of the Aviation/Space Writers Association, and the 1982 Donald T. Wright Award in Marine Transportation Journalism. A native of southern Illinois, Finley is a graduate of the University of Illinois at Champaign-Urbana.

❋ *Plate 63. Detail of plate 11.*

Design
Lazin & Katalan, N.Y.

Production Coordinator
Kelly Hall

Photography
David Talbott

Bruce Mann Photograph
Ralph Homan

Pattern Illustrations
Claude Martinot

Typography
Phoenix Typographers Inc., N.Y.

Printing
Commercial Lithographing Co.

The Kentucky Quilt Project, Inc.

Directors' Statement - 1991 - 1992

This catalogue, Kentucky Quilts 1800-1900, has been reprinted by The Kentucky Quilt Project, Inc. as part of its 1991-1992 project, "Louisville Celebrates the American Quilt." The celebration began in November, 1991, and continued through March, 1992. The Kentucky Quilt Project was formed in 1981 to survey the state's quilts. Its original directors were Shelly Zegart, Eleanor Bingham Miller, and Eunice Ray. Katy Christopherson organized the volunteers who aided that survey. It collected data for permanent reference on more than 1,000 quilts and exhibited some of the most interesting found in "Kentucky Quilts 1800-1900," which appeared first at the Louisville Museum of History and Science in 1983 and at 12 other museums thereafter under the auspices of the Smithsonian Institution Traveling Exhibition Service. Since 1981 groups in 48 states have undertaken quilt surveys informed by the methods and directions of The Kentucky Quilt Project. Other Project activities in the nineteen eighties included securing a Virginia Ivey quilt for Kentucky, bringing "The Artist and the Quilt" exhibition to Louisville, curating an exhibition of Kentucky quilts in Australia, and giving financial assistance to Kentucky quilt groups for special projects. It also acted as consultant for other state quilt surveys. In 1990 the current Directors of The Kentucky Quilt Project, Shelly Zegart, Eleanor Bingham Miller and Jonathan Holstein, began to discuss an appropriate way to celebrate the 20th anniversary of the historic exhibition, "Abstract Design in American Quilts," which opened at the Whitney Museum of American Art, New York, in 1971. The exhibition, curated by Jonathan Holstein and Gail van der Hoof, created a worldwide awareness of American quilts as designed objects. We decided a group of events which might illustrate and further the extraordinary developments in the field over the past two decades would be most beneficial. A recreation of the Whitney exhibition was a logical starting point, as many quilt researchers and scholars, quilt makers, collectors, and museum personnel now actively involved with quilts, never saw that original show. We planned also five other exhibitions, four conferences and additional associated events.

The exhibitions were: "Abstract Design in American Quilts" at the Louisville Museum of History and Science; "A Plain Aesthetic: Lancaster Amish Quilts" at the J.B. Speed Art Museum; "Always There: The African-American Presence in American Quilts" at the Louisville Museum of History and Science; "Quilts Now" at Zephyr Gallery; "Narrations: The Quilts of Yvonne Wells and Carolyn Mazloomi" at the Louisville Visual Art Association (Water Tower); and "Quilt Conceptions: Quilt Designs in Other Media" at the Kentucky Art and Craft Gallery. The four conferences were designed to further quilt scholarship in specific areas. "The African -American and the American Quilt" looked at African-American quilts both in relation to the African textile tradition and as part of the mainstream of American quilt making. "Directions in Quilt Scholarship" surveyed the field past and present, discussed quilts as art historical and social objects, and looked at problems in the field. "Quilts and Collections: Public, Private and Corporate" discussed the ways quilts are seen, collected and used by individual and corporate collectors, and museums. And "Toward an International Quilt Bibliography," through the individual efforts and interactions of 15 scholars, suggested the form and directions for a potential new quilt bibliography. Other events included lectures by scholars and quilt artists, and opportunities for participants to discuss issues in the field. In addition, data and dialogues developed at the conferences will be published, and audio and visual documentation of significant events were made for permanent record.

The Directors of The Kentucky Quilt Project hope the Celebration will bring, as did "Abstract Design in American Quilts" and The Kentucky Quilt Project's survey, new perspectives and directions to quilt scholarship, understanding and appreciation.

Shelly Zegart
Eleanor Bingham Miller
Jonathan Holstein

The Directors

The Kentucky Quilt Project, Inc. - 1991-1992

Jonathan Holstein wrote the introduction and quilt commentaries for The Kentucky Quilt Project's exhibition catalogue, Kentucky Quilts 1800-1900, in 1983 and became a Director in 1984. His work over the past several decades, collecting, creating exhibitions, writing and lecturing, has been seminal to the current understanding and appreciation of quilts. "Abstract Design in American Quilts," an exhibition he curated with Gail van der Hoof in 1971, showed quilts for the first time as designed objects and is universally noted as the starting point for the contemporary interest in quilts worldwide. Many other exhibitions here and abroad drawn from their collection gave wide circulation to their vision of quilts as aesthetic objects. His writing in the field began with the catalogue of the original Whitney Museum of American Art exhibition of "Abstract Design in American Quilts." His study of the background and design of American quilts, *The Pieced Quilt*, was published in 1973, and many articles and catalogues followed. He continues to write about quilts and has several books under way which he hopes to finish before the next millennium.

Shelly Zegart was a founder in 1981 of The Kentucky Quilt Project. Her initial collecting interest expanded with that state survey to a full-time professional involvement in the field. She collects, lectures, curates exhibitions, writes, advises other groups conducting state quilt surveys and sells fine quilts. Her articles have appeared in *The Quilt Digest*, *Antique Review* and other publications. She has curated many exhibitions here and abroad (including an exhibition of Kentucky quilts in Australia) and lectures on all aspects of quilt history and aesthetics.

Eleanor Bingham Miller's interest in quilts began with collecting. She was a founder of The Kentucky Quilt Project, organized in 1981 to survey her state's quilts, and has been active in all of its projects since. She is a filmmaker, and a partner in Double Play Productions, New York. In Louisville, her home, she serves the community in a number of positions, including the Boards of the J.B. Speed Art Museum and the Louisville Museum of History and Science.

Acknowledgments

The Kentucky Quilt Project, Inc. 1991-1992

We were helped significantly in achieving the extraordinary size and scope of this celebration by a most generous leadership gift from

Philip Morris Companies Inc.

We are deeply grateful to the following sources of support not only for financial assistance but also for the active interest and encouragement they lent to the project:

Mary and Barry Bingham, Sr. Fund
Rowland and Eleanor Bingham Miller Fund
Louisville Convention and Visitors Bureau
Brown-Forman Corporation
Citizens Fidelity Bank
James Graham Brown Foundation, Inc.

Significant contributions of time, energy, and finances by Jonathan Holstein, Eleanor Miller, Dorothy West and Shelly Zegart have been crucial to the realization of this project.

From the beginning of this project Dorothy West, Business Manager, and Kathy Mitchell-McGee, Project Coordinator, have been essential to every activity. Deep appreciation is also due JoAnn Gammon, Stacy Roof and Angela Messina for the constancy and strength of their commitment to this undertaking. Special thanks to David Roth, Alyssia Lazin and Theresa Mattei for their many years of association with The Kentucky Quilt Project and their significant work on this project – and to Velma Vaughn and Virginia Durkee for their invaluable assistance to Shelly Zegart and Jonathan Holstein.

Without the generous partnership of all the participating institutions, their boards of directors and staffs, this celebration would not have been possible. We want to warmly thank each institution's director for constant support of our efforts; Gail Becker, Museum of History and Science; Rita Steinberg, Kentucky Art and Craft Gallery; Peter Morrin, J.B. Speed Art Museum; and John Begley, Louisville Visual Art Association and also as representative of Zephyr Gallery.

No acknowledgments of support could be complete without mentioning our families, who tried to manage without us: Kenny Zegart, Rowland Miller, Cassia Holstein, Jared Holstein, Rowlie Miller, Worth Miller, Hannah Miller, Terri Zegart and Amy Zegart.